BJL
Siddur

Journeys Through the Siddur

ערב שבת Friday Evening

Torah Aura Productions

ISBN #1–891662–49–X

Torah Aura Productions • 4423 Fruitland Avenue, Los Angeles, CA 90058

(800) BE-Torah • (800) 238-6724 • (323) 585-7312 • fax (323) 585-0327

E-MAIL <misrad@torahaura.com> • Visit the Torah Aura website at www.torahaura.com

MANUFACTURED IN UNITED STATES OF AMERICA

Teaching *Journeys Through the Siddur*
An Introduction

This teacher's guide sets out the basic ideas and strategies for teaching *Journeys Through the Siddur: Friday Evening*. For more ideas and discussion with others who are using this material, go to **www.bb.torahaura.com**, and look for *Journeys Through the Siddur* under "Textbooks and How to Use Them".

Home Workbook Web site
www.jourevening.torahaura.com

At the Heart of This Book

The following six "huge ideas*" are at the heart of the design of this book. They should be at the center of the focus that every teacher brings to this material.

1. When we study "prayers" it is important that we also work on "the art of prayer."

Prayer is something that happens in the heart and the mind and not just the mouth. It is communication with the self, communication within a community and communication with God. If we only learn how to say words in the Siddur but have no way of letting the words work inside us, then we are like someone who knows how to turn on a computer on which no programs have been installed.

Journeys Through the Siddur: Friday Evening intentionally combines work on (a) performing prayers, (b) mastering some of the Hebrew language used in prayers, and (c) providing students with windows into the ways that prayers come to have personal meaning.

2. Stories form a window into the process of prayer.

The Rabbis believed that the Siddur was a lot like the script that an actor uses. For them, prayer was the capturing of a moment when the Jewish people had a unique experience of the Divine. When we use the Siddur (and can read it in the context of the stories of these moments) we can be just like actors using our own experiences to recreate the moments. The Siddur is really an opportunity to relive the most important moments of the Jewish experience.

Journeys Through the Siddur: Friday Evening collects these stories and invites students to use them to find the connection between these focal Jewish moments and their own life experiences and understanding.

3. Knowing and recognizing word-parts, roots and other language elements evolves a strong connection to the liturgy.

Even when we do not have time to teach our students to speak Hebrew, even when we will not be able to give them enough vocabulary and grammar to accurately translate Hebrew texts, we still have the ability to give them a sense of the meaning of the Hebrew in the Siddur.

This curriculum uses a technique called the "the approximation of translation" that teaches students a core Hebrew vocabulary, builds their skill at recognizing roots in context, and then challenges them to use those tools to build an evolving sense of "the general meaning" of key passages in the Siddur. When students sense a growing ability to "understand" the Siddur, their connection deepens.

---

*IF YOU ARE FAMILIAR WITH "UNDERSTANDING BY DESIGN," THESE ARE OUR "ENDURING UNDERSTANDINGS."

"Sounding" is the process of looking at letters on a page and pronouncing the "words" they form. Sounding is an enabling tool that lets us move to the other two levels.

"Reading" is the act of looking at letters on a page and deriving meaning from them. This is one way that the liturgy comes off the page and enters our heart.

"Performing" is the process of repeatedly practicing a given passage until its words can be spoken or sung with reasonable fluency. "Performing" is a skill that enables most participation in Jewish worship. Students will use "sounding" to learn pieces of their bar/bat mitzvah material, but the rest of their Jewish life will primarily require mastered performances.

This curriculum spends some time building sounding skills and works toward reading but centers on the performance of the prayers.

In this curriculum we avoid the word "reading" when meaning is not involved. In this guide we will bow to conventional usage and use the term "decoding" to refer to "sounding."

Jewish worship has formal structures. When students know the pattern, order and sequence of the prayers (a) they know where they are in the service at any time, (b) the presence of each element makes sense, and (c) they have a better chance of being able to surf the flow of the liturgy and create meaningful personal experiences.

Journeys Through the Siddur: Friday Evening is designed to make the structure, location, interconnection and purpose of each prayer clear. Each prayer is clearly identified as a piece of a structure. Its context and function are always clearly presented.

Lifelong learning requires the building of connections, insights and tools. There is much more liturgy to be mastered than can be studied in the context of most schools. We therefore need to provide our students with tools that they can continue to apply after our classes have finished.

Journeys Through the Siddur: Friday Evening teaches students to (a) recognize the structure and position of prayers inside services, (b) use roots and other language elements to gain a sense of their meaning and (c) use the stories and insights of the rabbinical tradition to develop their own "art of prayer."

Journeys Through the Siddur: Friday Evening is designed to be one of four books in a student's journey through his or her formal Jewish learning. It presupposes that the students have already completed a reading primer and have mastered the basic "reading code." While it would be helpful if students have begun to build a foundation of Hebrew vocabulary, this is not a prerequisite for success with this material. As the teacher, you can adjust the extent to which you reinforce vocabulary through games, review sheets and other teaching strategies.

Journeys Through the Siddur: Friday Evening has been designed to fit into the Torah Aura school curriculum. *BJL Beginnings* can be used in kindergarten or first grade. *Now I Know my Alef Bet* is a first-year preprimer. It is designed to teach both letter recognition and a basic vocabulary. *Marilyn Price and Friends Learn the Alef Bet from Alef to Tav* is the second preprimer that both grow "sounding" skills through the introduction of vowels and reinforces vocabulary. *Ot la-Ba'ot* (Signs of the Future) or *Tiyulim* (*Journeys: A Hebrew Primer*) are our primers. They grows directly out the previous progression of books and teach the complete sounding code, core Hebrew vocabulary and even the history of the Hebrew language. The three volumes of *Journeys Through the Siddur* have been engineered to grow out of that work. If you will be teaching *Journeys Through the Siddur: Friday Evening*, reviewing the previous material is a good idea.

You are a very lucky teacher. This year you will have the opportunity to move your students beyond the basics and into the world of meaningful Jewish prayer and practice. You will give your students the tools they need to become active meaning makers and participants in the ritual life of the Jewish people.

Journeys Through the Siddur: Friday Evening is designed to provide you with the materials you need to enable your students to successfully achieve four major goals.

- **Your students will be able to perform the basic prayers from the Torah service and concluding prayers of the Friday evening service.** By mastering these skills, your students will feel comfortable participating in the services in your synagogue. They will feel at home not only in your synagogue but also in any synagogue. They will never feel left out of the Jewish community.

- **Your students will develop an understanding of the generalized meaning of these basic prayers.** They will learn the overall meaning of the prayer as well as the meaning of words and phrases. They will develop sensitivity to translation and will be able to tell when the English translation in the Siddur (prayerbook) is close to the meaning of the Hebrew or is a poetic adaptation.

- **Your students will explore the personal meaning in these prayers.** They will be able to express the ways in which the stories underlying each prayer are connected to something in their own lives. As they recite or chant the words of the prayers they will be able to draw upon the stories so that the prayers come from their hearts.

- **Your students will extend their knowledge of how the Hebrew language operates.** They will grow their passive vocabulary and learn elements of grammar such as prefixes, roots and suffixes so that they will be able to extend their understanding of Hebrew. They will know enough words and analytical skills to be able to make sense of what many prayers say.

Achieving these goals will have a lifelong impact on your students. Under your guidance, your students will grow not only in mind but also in spirit. With your help, they will gain knowledge, understanding and insights so that they can begin to take the next steps in becoming active and committed Jews.

We will be here to support you every important step of the way. You may always call 800 BE-TORAH and ask for a consultation. You have a standing invitation to e-mail misrad@torahaura.com with suggestions, questions and problems. This teacher's guide, vocabulary posters, flashcards, Class Workbook and Home Workbook with a website support this material.

When you first look at *Journeys Through the Siddur: Friday Evening* you will notice that it is not quite like other Siddur (prayerbook) texts you may have used. That is because we are interested in both the mastery (performance) and the meaning (personal connection) of the prayers. We have built *Journeys Through the Siddur: Friday Evening* posters and flashcards to be very much like other Siddur resources with some wonderful new elements. To use this book you need to find a way of being comfortable with a few new techniques. Then it will be easy to step up from what you have been using to this book.

Shabbat on Wednesday

Rabbi Elimelekh and Rabbi Zusya were brothers who were Ḥasidic Rabbis. Often they would spend Shabbat together. Together, they would create a wonderful Shabbat experience. Once, Rabbi Elimelekh confessed, "Brother, I am not sure that the feeling I get on Shabbat is a real Shabbat spirit." Rabbi Zusya told him, "I am worried about the same thing." The two of them decided to try an experiment. They decided to create Shabbat on a weekday. If they felt the same way they did every Shabbat, then they weren't getting a real Shabbat spirit. They made a great Shabbat meal. They put on their Shabbat clothes and the fur hats they wore on Shabbat. They sang Shabbat songs and celebrated. Both of them had an amazing experience. It felt just as holy as Shabbat did.

The brothers were upset. They were sure that what they had been feeling on Shabbat was not the real Shabbat feeling. They went to Dov Baer, the Holy Maggid. They asked him, "How can we get to feel the real Shabbat feeling? He told them. "If you prepared and welcomed Shabbat, if you put on your Shabbat clothes and the fur hats you wore, what you felt was a Shabbat experience even though it was a weekday. Your actions brought the light of Shabbat down to earth." (retold from Martin Buber, *Tales of the Ḥasidim*)

Questions
1. What made the weekday feel like Shabbat?
2. What brings the light of Shabbat down to you?
3. How can knowing this story help you point your heart when you enter קַבָּלַת שַׁבָּת?

6

comfortable with a few new techniques. Then it will be easy to step up from what you have been using to this book.

1. **TEACHING WITH STORIES:** *Journeys Through the Siddur* is loaded with stories (in English) from the Talmud, the Midrash and folk literature. These stories are all designed to provide a path for each student to build a personal meaning for each prayer. Stories are really good at doing that because they both relate and create real life experience. Working with stories is fairly easy. In this case we can recommend a simple three-part process.

   a. *Convey the story.* This can be done in a number of ways: (a) You can tell the story. (b) You can read the story. (c) Students can read the story silently alone or in small groups of two or three. Our single recommendation is that you do not call on students to read the story out loud. That process can be both slow and tedious. However, Erica Dorf, one of our master teachers who helped us develop this curriculum, regularly reads the story to her class, pausing for the whole class to read key lines or words in the story.

   b. *Allow the students to interpret the story.* This involves first asking a couple of questions to make sure that students "heard" or "got" the story. For example, you might ask, "What problem did the Baal Shem have?" "How did Potiphar solve his problem?" etc. These lead up to the "real" question we care about. The core question is "What do you think this story teaches?" "What lessons can you learn from this story?" When you ask the core questions, you need to make two things clear: first, that you are not looking for a single right answer, and second, that there are a number of answers you can learn from a given story. This allows you to listen to a number of different student opinions.

   Know that it is a good technique to respond to every answer by restating it in your own words to show that you were listening and to clarify the idea for the class. It is good to ask the student a question or two—or make a comment or two—about the answer. This could be "You know that one of the prayers says exactly what you said, 'that God creates new things every day.'" Or "You said that a minyan can do things a single person cannot do. What about a minyan makes a difference?"

   c. *Share your own opinion or clarification.* I tell lots of stories every week. I invite lots of groups to share their own meanings. One of the lessons I have learned is that the meaning I want, the meaning I think is obvious, almost never comes out. People always hear their own things in stories, often wonderful things that I have not noticed. The previous step of this process is your opportunity to enjoy your students' creativity. This step belongs to you. Having heard all of the other opinions, you now have your opportunity to share or to explain. Here is where you can say "Here is something else to learn from this story..." Here is where you can push the story into meaning(s) that relate to the lesson without denying any of the meanings your class has found.

   d. *Give students practice in "pointing their hearts".* The last question we ask about almost every story is "How can knowing this story help you know where to point your heart when you say the given prayer?" This is a hard question for your students because it is different than questions they have been asked in other places. It is a new kind of thinking. Do not model answers to this question (once you have given them time to answer). You will be surprised to see that in two or three stories they will get the process and often even anticipate the question.

2. **INTRODUCING VOCABULARY:** One of the secrets of this curriculum is that we are trying to build a large passive vocabulary. A passive vocabulary is one that students can recognize, not necessarily one that students can use. In other words, we want them to know that קָדוֹש means "holy," not know that the Hebrew word for "holy" is קָדוֹש. Passive is much easier than active.

We will be using a limited number of words a lot of times, trying to make as many of them familiar as possible. This is not the same as regularly drilling and testing for "vocabulary mastery."

The bottom line is this: The more words that "stick," the more meaning Hebrew prayers will have. The more words that have meaning, the stronger connection there will be with the Siddur.

Each unit uses a limited number of words. If you turn to the last page in each unit you will find a "review" page. This page will list the major words, roots and language elements (prefixes and suffixes, etc.) that will be used in the course of the unit. The more frequently these are used and reviewed, the deeper they will sink in.

The best way of introducing (and drilling) vocabulary is with 5½" by 8½" posters. A set of these will be available from Torah Aura shortly after the release of this book. You are also free to make your own. Each of these cards has an "icon"—the graphic image that prompts the word on one side and the Hebrew on the other. Both sides can be used playfully in class for both introduction and review.

It is good to introduce new words and review key words at the beginning of each lesson.

3. **MAINTAINING AN "ACTIVE" VOCABULARY:** There are two distinct skills we care about. One is knowing the meaning of individual words. This is seeing the picture of a king and knowing that the Hebrew word is מֶלֶךְ, and this is seeing the Hebrew word מֶלֶךְ and knowing that it means "a king." The second skill is recognizing the root מֶלֶךְ in context. The prayer goes: יִמְלֹךְ יי לְעוֹלָם אֱלֹהַיִךְ צִיּוֹן

When students can suddenly see צִיּוֹן, אֱלֹהִים, עוֹלָם, יי, מֶלֶךְ in the sentence and get the sense that "King Forever Adonai God of/in צִיּוֹן," then that is a huge deal. The prayer has now made sense.

We move toward these two skills with two teaching techniques:

   a. *Regular review and drill* (with mini-posters and exercises) of the core vocabulary that is indicated as significant.

   b. *"On location"* vocabulary work. This is done by pointing out words, roots and forms that have been learned in random reading exercises, in services and in other contexts. The purpose here is to move from exercises into real Siddur (and text) situations.

4. **APPROXIMATING TRANSLATIONS:** There are two goals in *Journeys Through the Siddur: Friday Evening* that you will not find in other Siddur curricula—at least they are not taught intentionally in other texts. However, we feel that these goals are critical if we are going to enable our students to "make meaning" of the prayers they recite. These goals are:

   a. *Being able to match the English translation to the Hebrew.* It is a wonderful moment when you are sitting in services with your class and one of your students suddenly comes to you and says, "This English translation doesn't seem to come from the Hebrew. How come?"

   b. *To get a sense of the general idea of a passage.* In a world where we do not have enough time to teach Hebrew grammar, to carefully build understandings of tense, form, etc., our students are not going to master enough Hebrew to do accurate translations, but we can help them to get the general idea of a passage. However, the skill of "sort of knowing the gist" builds a sense of connection to Hebrew prayers that pure sounding skills don't.

There is a whole series of exercises in the book that calls for approximation of translation. They all have a bar with key vocabulary and a box with other word elements. The directions ask students to state "my best guess at the meaning of this prayer". The job for the students is to utilize the given information, take their experience and put these pieces together to express a sense of the prayer. This is exactly what we hope students will do when they sit in services.

Here is one set of strategies to use for these exercises:

(i) Let students work in small groups (two or three) to make their best guesses at a translation. Make sure that everyone knows that this is "guessing" and not "expecting."

(ii) Have the class share various translations. You may even want to write them on the board.

(iii) Extend the learning by first showing the things that the class (or individuals) got right. Then go over the pieces that were hard, or unclear, or even done incorrectly. Be sure to use the elements the students have contributed to build a relatively accurate translation.

The key here is that everyone knows that the class is using the knowledge they have in order to come close to a reasonable translation and that they are not failing at getting a translation right. Indeed, every translation is only an approximation of the original language, and there is rarely only one official "right way". Think of a child wrestling with a parent. The child will not win. But the child can do well, and both of them can have fun.

Our purpose here is not to empower students to accurately translate large portions of the Siddur. We want them to gain a sense of connection to the Hebrew text—to begin to develop a sense of what the prayers mean on a phrase-by-phrase basis. Working with roots, applying word parts, struggling to wrestle the Hebrew into a sense of English meaning makes that connection and helps to deeply root the vocabulary and the process. We work with one or two verses—never the whole prayer. We don't expect teachers to test "mastery" on their quizzes and exams. Rather, we are practicing a harder skill in order to achieve a working memory of vocabulary and very basic grammar.

Journeys Through the Siddur: Friday Evening has been carefully designed and edited to enable you to complete the material within a normal school year in either a one-day-a-week school or a two-day-a-week school with time constraints. The book is divided into 23 lessons. Each lesson is designed to be teachable in a forty-five- to fifty-minute period.

הַשְׁכִּיבֵנוּ

Let us lie down in PEACE, ADONAI, our God,	1. הַשְׁכִּיבֵנוּ יי אֱלֹהֵינוּ לְשָׁלוֹם,
and then let us stand back up alive, our Ruler,	2. וְהַעֲמִידֵנוּ מַלְכֵּנוּ לְחַיִּים,
and spread over us a Sukkah of YOUR Peace	3. וּפְרוֹשׂ עָלֵינוּ סֻכַּת שְׁלוֹמֶךָ,
and fix us with good advice before You,	4. וְתַקְּנֵנוּ בְּעֵצָה טוֹבָה מִלְּפָנֶיךָ,
and save us for Your own NAME's sake.	5. וְהוֹשִׁיעֵנוּ לְמַעַן שְׁמֶךָ.
Protect us, Side with us, and turn away from us	6. וְהָגֵן בַּעֲדֵנוּ, וְהָסֵר מֵעָלֵינוּ
ENEMIES, SICKNESS, the SWORD, HUNGER and SORROW	7. אוֹיֵב דֶּבֶר וְחֶרֶב וְרָעָב וְיָגוֹן,
and turn away Satan from before us and from behind us	8. וְהָסֵר שָׂטָן מִלְּפָנֵינוּ וּמֵאַחֲרֵינוּ,
and shelter us in the shadow of Your wings	9. וּבְצֵל כְּנָפֶיךָ תַּסְתִּירֵנוּ,
Because You are God, The ONE Who guards and rescues us.	10. כִּי אֵל שׁוֹמְרֵנוּ וּמַצִּילֵנוּ אָתָּה,
Because You are God, the Gracious and Merciful Ruler.	11. כִּי אֵל מֶלֶךְ חַנּוּן וְרַחוּם אָתָּה.
the ONE Who guards us in our GOINGS and COMINGS	12. שְׁמוֹר צֵאתֵנוּ וּבוֹאֵנוּ
in LIFE and in PEACE	13. לְחַיִּים וּלְשָׁלוֹם
forever and always	14. מֵעַתָּה וְעַד עוֹלָם.
BLESSED be You, ADONAI,	15. בָּרוּךְ אַתָּה יי
The ONE Who spreads a Sukkah of Peace over us	16. הַפּוֹרֵשׂ סֻכַּת שָׁלוֹם עָלֵינוּ
and over all of the nation Israel	17. וְעַל כָּל עַמּוֹ יִשְׂרָאֵל
and on Jerusalem.	18. וְעַל יְרוּשָׁלָיִם.

47

Unlike many other Hebrew workbooks, *Journeys Through the Siddur: Friday Evening* does not base its instruction on isolated nonsense syllables. Except for a few game formats, all of the Hebrew the students will encounter will be in the form of meaningful words, phrases and sentences. As part of your warm-up activities, be sure to include whole word as well as part-to-whole sounding practice. Vocabulary posters that will be available through Torah Aura and coordinated with this textbook will be very helpful.

Americans often call the act of looking at Hebrew letters and pronouncing them without any comprehension "READING" or "MECHANICAL READING." The simple truth is that in real language education, "READING" has to do with "MEANING" and "SOUNDING" has to do with pronunciation. We will use words like "sound" or "practice" in this teacher's guide for two reasons. (1) It keeps us honest as teachers about what we are and are not accomplishing.

Psalms

Practice these words and phrases from קַבָּלַת שַׁבָּת.

1.	אוֹר לֵב לְהַר שִׂמְחָה שָׁלוֹם כִּי יִתֵּן
2.	הָאָרֶץ קָדוֹשׁ הַיָּם יְבָרֵךְ יִרְעַם לְצוּר זֶרַע
3.	לְכוּ לַצַּדִּיק לְעַמּוֹ וְלִישְׁרֵי קָדְשׁוֹ
4.	יִשְׂמְעוּ יִרְעַם נְרַנְּנָה רוֹמְמוּ וְהִשְׁתַּחֲווּ יִשְׂמָחוּ
5. Psalm 95	לְכוּ נְרַנְּנָה לַיי נָרִיעָה לְצוּר יִשְׁעֵנוּ.
6. Psalm 96	יִשְׂמְחוּ הַשָּׁמַיִם וְתָגֵל הָאָרֶץ, יִרְעַם הַיָּם וּמְלֹאוֹ.
7. Psalm 97	אוֹר זָרֻעַ לַצַּדִּיק, וּלְיִשְׁרֵי לֵב שִׂמְחָה.
8. Psalm 99	רוֹמְמוּ יי אֱלֹהֵינוּ, וְהִשְׁתַּחֲווּ לְהַר קָדְשׁוֹ.
9. Psalm 99	כִּי קָדוֹשׁ יי אֱלֹהֵינוּ.
10. Psalm 29	יי עֹז לְעַמּוֹ יִתֵּן, יי יְבָרֵךְ אֶת-עַמּוֹ בַשָּׁלוֹם.

4

(2) It minimizes the frustration that many students feel when they realize that they have learned to "sound out Hebrew" and have not actually learned Hebrew.

We've all done it, both as students and as teachers. When faced with lines of practice sounding material, we've taken turns sounding aloud in "round robin" fashion. And almost all of us can admit that this practice was not the most enjoyable way to learn. If we were not confident sounders, we cringed whenever we were asked to sound aloud without a chance to rehearse; in fact, we often spent so much time and effort trying to figure out when and what we would be asked to sound that we lost our place. At the very least, we didn't learn anything while the other students were sounding. If we were confident sounders, we found it uncomfortable to listen while others struggled and often became bored. There has to be a better way!

The key is to identify exactly what our goals are in sounding practice. We want all of our students to become fluent and confident sounders. In order to develop strong sounding skills, we assume that students need lots of practice. We need to find ways in which all students get sufficient repetitions supported by correct modeling. We need to keep in mind that some students will need more practice than others, as well as the fact that some students prefer to practice privately before sounding in front of a large group.

Whenever you encounter a page of sounding practice in *Journeys Through the Siddur*, try to create learning structures that enable the largest number of students possible to engage in active sounding with correct modeling, so that your students can develop confidence without threat of embarrassment. (In other words, try to avoid situations in which only one child is sounding at a time and is making mistakes in front of the whole class.) Here are some suggestions.

As you introduce each new line, sound it aloud to your students, and have them follow the sounding by putting a finger on each word. As you get to know your class, you will be able to determine if you need to repeat the modeling more than once.

After you have finished modeling, have the students sound it out along with you, again using their fingers to mark the place. As you get to know your class, you will be able to determine how many times you need to repeat the choral sounding.

Have your students take turns listening to each other practice. As you get to know your class, you will be able to determine which students make good pairs. You may ask some of the weaker students to be your practice buddies so that you can give them more individualized attention.

Ask your principal if you can have a listening center for your class. This can be as simple as a small tape recorder with headphones. Record a sounding exercise or passage, speaking clearly and at an appropriate speed, slightly slower than normal conversation but not so slow that the words or phrases become distorted. Clearly identify the lines and pages that you are reading. Make sure that the student listening to the tape is following along with the written material and is moving a finger along as each word is spoken.

Building in sufficient "wait time" whenever you ask a question or require students to perform is one easy and effective modification that you can make whenever and whatever you teach. Allow time for silent reading and silent practice, and you will be pleased with the results. Let students indicate to you when they feel ready to read aloud.

After students have had time to practice silently and/or practice with their buddy, you can bring the class back together and ask each student to read a section of his or her choice. If everyone seems to be avoiding a particular line or section, you could suggest a choral performance.

For more alternatives to "round-robin" drill, see *Good-bye Round Robin: 25 Effective Oral Reading Strategies*, Michael F. Opits and Timothy V. Rasinski (Portsmouth, NH: Heinemann, 1998).

Blank Page

X

Journeys Through the Siddur

עֶרֶב שַׁבָּת Friday Evening

Table of Contents

ISBN #1-891662-38-4

Copyright © 2004 Torah Aura Productions

All rights reserved. No part of this publication may be reproduced or transmitted in any form or by any means graphic, electronic or mechanical, including photocopying, recording or by any information storage and retrieval system, without permission in writing from the publisher.

Torah Aura Productions ◆ 4423 Fruitland Avenue, Los Angeles, CA 90058

(800) BE-Torah ◆ (800) 238-6724 ◆ (323) 585-7312 ◆ fax (323) 585-0327

E-MAIL <misrad@torahaura.com> ◆ Visit the Torah Aura website at www.torahaura.com

MANUFACTURED IN CHINA

קַבָּלַת שַׁבָּת

Lesson 1

Blank Page

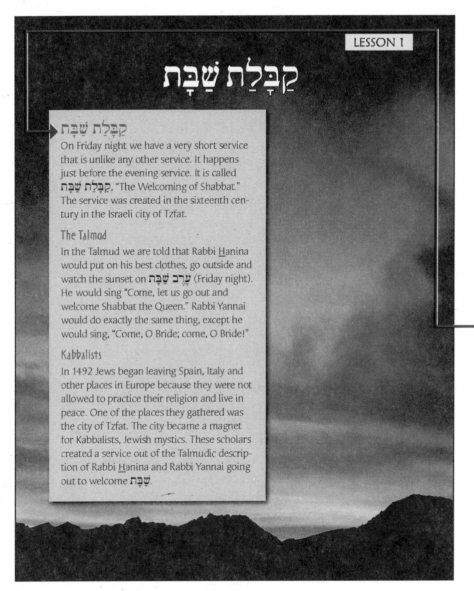

קַבָּלַת שַׁבָּת

קַבָּלַת שַׁבָּת

On Friday night we have a very short service that is unlike any other service. It happens just before the evening service. It is called קַבָּלַת שַׁבָּת, "The Welcoming of Shabbat." The service was created in the sixteenth century in the Israeli city of Tzfat.

The Talmud

In the Talmud we are told that Rabbi Ḥanina would put on his best clothes, go outside and watch the sunset on עֶרֶב שַׁבָּת (Friday night). He would sing "Come, let us go out and welcome Shabbat the Queen." Rabbi Yannai would do exactly the same thing, except he would sing, "Come, O Bride; come, O Bride!"

Kabbalists

In 1492 Jews began leaving Spain, Italy and other places in Europe because they were not allowed to practice their religion and live in peace. One of the places they gathered was the city of Tzfat. The city became a magnet for Kabbalists, Jewish mystics. These scholars created a service out of the Talmudic description of Rabbi Ḥanina and Rabbi Yannai going out to welcome שַׁבָּת.

LESSON 1: INTRODUCTION

These are the core concepts of קַבָּלַת שַׁבָּת.

Big Idea

1. The קַבָּלַת שַׁבָּת service welcomes Shabbat.
2. The origins of קַבָּלַת שַׁבָּת are in Talmudic stories about Rabbi Ḥanina and Rabbi Yannai.
3. The Kabbalists of Tzfat expanded the Talmudic description and created the קַבָּלַת שַׁבָּת service in a fuller form.

Learning Activities

1. Introducing the unit
2. Exploring the themes
3. Reviewing the key themes

You Know You've Succeeded When...

1. Students can describe the purpose of the קַבָּלַת שַׁבָּת service.
2. Students can describe the simple Talmudic origins of קַבָּלַת שַׁבָּת.
3. Students can describe the Kabbalisitic expansion of the קַבָּלַת שַׁבָּת service.

1. Introducing the Unit ■ LOOK at the קַבָּלַת שַׁבָּת Service in the siddur. Find out that it is made up of six Psalms (one for each day of the week) and לְכָה דוֹדִי. (Some siddurim have a few more parts—some Reform services have fewer parts).

2. Exploring the Themes ■ CONVEY THE INFORMATION IN THE INTRODUCTION: Do one of the following. [a] DESCRIBE the information to your students. [b] READ out loud and DISCUSS this information or [c] ASSIGN your students to READ the information on their own and then DISCUSS it.

3. Reviewing the Key Themes ■

Here are the big points you want to communicate:

- Shabbat begins with a welcoming service, קַבָּלַת שַׁבָּת.
- Two Talmudic Rabbis created personal welcoming services in which they called Shabbat a "queen" and a "bride."
- The Kabbalists of Tzfat turned this into a bigger ceremony.

This page has students practice words and phrases from that Psalms that appear in the
קַבָּלַת שַׁבָּת service.

- Practice is good.

- Rehearsal/Performance

- Students successfully perform these texts.

- **Rehearsal/Performance** Students work in *hevruta* pairs rehearsing the words
and phrases on this page before performing them.

Psalms

Practice these words and phrases from קַבָּלַת שַׁבָּת.

1. יִתֵּן   כִּי   שָׁלוֹם   שִׂמְחָה   לְהַר   לֵב   אוֹר

2. זֶרַע   לְצוּר   יִרְעַם   יְבָרֵךְ   הַיָּם   קָדוֹשׁ   הָאָרֶץ

3. קָדְשׁוֹ   וּלְיִשְׁרֵי   הַשָּׁמַיִם   לְעַמּוֹ   לַצַּדִּיק   לְכוּ

4. יִשְׂמְחוּ   וְהִשְׁתַּחֲווּ   רוֹמְמוּ   נְרַנְּנָה   יִרְעַם   יִשְׁעֵנוּ

5. לְכוּ נְרַנְּנָה לַיי נָרִיעָה לְצוּר יִשְׁעֵנוּ.   Psalm 95

6. יִשְׂמְחוּ הַשָּׁמַיִם וְתָגֵל הָאָרֶץ, יִרְעַם הַיָּם וּמְלֹאוֹ.   Psalm 96

7. אוֹר זָרֻעַ לַצַּדִּיק, וּלְיִשְׁרֵי לֵב שִׂמְחָה.   Psalm 97

8. רוֹמְמוּ יי אֱלֹהֵינוּ, וְהִשְׁתַּחֲווּ לְהַר קָדְשׁוֹ   Psalm 99

9. כִּי קָדוֹשׁ יי אֱלֹהֵינוּ.   Psalm 99

10. יי עֹז לְעַמּוֹ יִתֵּן, יי יְבָרֵךְ אֶת-עַמּוֹ בַשָּׁלוֹם.   Psalm 29

4

TRANSLATION

Review the vocabulary and make your best guess at the meaning of the this line of רוֹמְמוּ from Psalm 99.

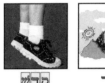

קָדַשׁ   הַר   שָׁחָה   רוֹם

Your teacher will help you with your translation.

רוֹמְמוּ יי אֱלֹהֵינוּ וְהִשְׁתַּחֲווּ לְהַר קָדְשׁוֹ
כִּי קָדוֹשׁ יי אֱלֹהֵינוּ

Adonai our God is high

And bow down to the mountain of His holiness

Because Holy is Adonai our God

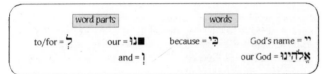

word parts		words	
to/for = לְ	our = נוּ■	because = כִּי	God's name = יי
	and = וְ		our God = אֱלֹהֵינוּ

5

TRANSLATION/CHOREOGRAPHY

This page has students work on a translation of part of רוֹמְמוּ.

Big Ideas

1. Growing and reinforcing Hebrew vocabulary leads to a growing affinity with the liturgy.

2. Applying the Hebrew they have to form rough translations of Hebrew prayers (a) helps students to feel closer to those texts, (b) reinforces the Hebrew they are learning and (c) develops a process they can continue to apply to the Siddur.

Learning Activities

1. Introducing/reviewing vocabulary
2. Working out a trial translation
3. Correcting translations
4. Prayer drill

You Know You've Succeeded When...

1 Students work out a reasonable translation of this text.
2. Students correct their translation.

1. Introducing/Reviewing Vocabulary ■ [a] Using VOCABULARY POSTERS and FLASHCARDS, the teacher should introduce and drill the core vocabulary needed for this translation. [b] Some game playing or team competition is the perfect way to reinforce this vocabulary.

2. Working out a Trial Translation ■ [a] Working in pairs, students should develop their own best TRANSLATION of this text. [b] They should not worry about being perfect—they should worry about coming close. EXPECT a working translation something like:
Adonai our God is high
And bow down to the mountain of His holiness
Because Holy is Adonai our God

3. Correcting Translations ■
[a] רוֹמְמוּ actually means You (pl) Lift up Adonai.
[b] It is not a translation issue, but הַר קָדְשׁוֹ can be both Sinai and the Temple Mount.

4. Prayer Drill ■ Practice performing this portion of the prayer. SING or READ it together.

SHABBAT ON WEDNESDAY

Two brothers manage to create a "real Shabbat feeling" on a weekday because their preparation for Shabbat was so sincere.

Big Ideas

1. Preparation helps to create Shabbat.
2. It was possible for two holy rabbis to prepare well enough to create Shabbat on a weekday.

Learning Activities

1. Read the story
2. Go over the story in hevruta.
3. Discuss the questions

You Know You've Succeeded When...

1. Students can retell the story.
2. Students can provide reasonable answers to the questions.

1. Read the Story ■

2. Go over the Story in Hevruta ■

3. Discuss the Questions ■

1. **What made the weekday feel like Shabbat?** The quality of spiritual preparation that they made for Shabbat.

2. **What brings the light of Shabbat down to you?** This question invites students to give personal answers such as "my family," "my mother's cooking," etc.

3. **How can knowing this story help you point your heart when you enter Kabbalat Shabbat?** Ideally, "My preparation for Shabbat can effect my Shabbat experience."

Shabbat on Wednesday

Rabbi Elimelekh and Rabbi Zusya were brothers who were Hasidic Rabbis. Often they would spend Shabbat together. Together, they would create a wonderful Shabbat experience. Once, Rabbi Elimelekh confessed, "Brother, I am not sure that the feeling I get on Shabbat is a real Shabbat spirit." Rabbi Zusya told him, "I am worried about the same thing." The two of them decided to try an experiment. They decided to create Shabbat on a weekday. If they felt the same way they did every Shabbat, then they weren't getting a real Shabbat spirit. They made a great Shabbat meal. They put on their Shabbat clothes and the fur hats they wore on Shabbat. They sang Shabbat songs and celebrated. Both of them had an amazing experience. It felt just as holy as Shabbat did.

The brothers were upset. They were sure that what they had been feeling on Shabbat was not the real Shabbat feeling. They went to Dov Baer, the Holy Maggid. They asked him, "How can we get to feel the real Shabbat feeling? He told them. "If you prepared and welcomed Shabbat, if you put on your Shabbat clothes and Shabbat hats, then what you felt was a Shabbat experience even though it was a weekday. Your actions brought the light of Shabbat down to earth." (retold from Martin Buber, *Tales of the Hasidim*)

Questions
1. What made the weekday feel like Shabbat?
2. What brings the light of Shabbat down to you?
3. How can knowing this story help you point your heart when you enter קַבָּלַת שַׁבָּת?

6

לְכָה דוֹדִי

Lesson 2

This lesson introduces לְכָה דוֹדִי. It includes:

Blank Page

לְכָה דוֹדִי

LESSON 2

Rabbi Shlomo ha-Levy, a Kabbalist from Tzfat, wrote a song to use at this service. It is לְכָה דוֹדִי.

Some things to know about לְכָה דוֹדִי:

• It has nine verses; eight of them spell out Shlomo ha-Levy's name in the first letter of each verse.

• It calls שַׁבָּת both a queen and a bride.

   • It talks about three things: Shabbat, Jerusalem, and the Redemption. (The Redemption is when God finally helps us to fix the world and make it into a place that is good for everyone.)

שַׁבָּת the Bride

שַׁבָּת went crying to God, saying, "I am all alone." She explained, "Every other day of the week has its own partner. Sunday has Monday. Tuesday has Wednesday. Thursday has Friday. I am the only one who is alone." God said to her, "Don't worry. The Families-of-Israel will be your partner" (Genesis Rabbah 11.8).

The idea of the שַׁבָּת as a bride comes from this story. How can the community of Israel and a day of the week be partners?

LESSON 2: INTRODUCTION

These are the core concepts of לְכָה דוֹדִי.

Big Ideas

1. Shabbat takes welcoming. Jews evolved customs to welcome Shabbat.

2. לְכָה דוֹדִי grew out of the Talmud and was shaped and molded by Kabbalists who lived in Tzfat in the 16th century.

3. לְכָה דוֹדִי merges three images, (a) Shabbat, (b) the rebuilding of Jerusalem and (c) the redemption.

Learning Activities

1. Introducing the unit
2. Exploring the themes
3. Reviewing the key themes

You Know You've Succeeded When...

1. Students can retell the story.
2. Student can provide reasonable answers to the questions.

1. **Introducing the Unit** ■ Introduce the idea of the Kabbalists going out to the fields to welcome Shabbat. Ask students to imagine themselves going out to meet the Shabbat bride on Friday afternoon. Ask if they have rituals any of their own for greeting Shabbat.

2. **Exploring the Themes** ■ CONVEY THE INFORMATION IN THE INTRODUCTION: Do one of the following. [a] DESCRIBE the information to your students. [b] READ out loud and DISCUSS this information or [c] ASSIGN your students to READ the information on their own and then DISCUSS it.

3. **Reviewing the Key Themes** ■

Here are the big points you want to communicate:

• Shabbat begins with a welcoming service, קַבָּלַת שַׁבָּת.

• Two talmudic rabbis created personal welcoming services in which they called Shabbat a "queen" and a "bride."

• The Kabbalists of Tzfat turned this into a bigger ceremony.

• The song/poem לְכָה דוֹדִי was created for this ceremony.

• It combines the images of (a) welcoming Shabbat, (b) rebuilding Jerusalem and (c) the coming of the messiah/final redemption.

TRANSLATION AND TEXT

This page contains the Hebrew and English text of the לְכָה דוֹדִי. It should be used for both introducing the prayer and practicing and perfecting its performance.

Big Ideas

1. When we enable students to perfect performances of the core liturgy we make it possible for them to far more easily participate in communal worship.

2. By scanning the English of prayers students can grow insights into the meaning of the liturgy.

Learning Activities

1. Scanning the English text
2. Practicing the Hebrew text

You Know You've Succeeded When...

1. Students describe insights gained from looking at the English text.
2. Students practice their performance of the Hebrew text.

1. Scanning the English Text ■ INVITE students to SCAN the English translation of these prayers. ASK them what "big ideas" they can find by looking. Because this is a poem, it is harder than any English we have looked at before. You can make it much easier by breaking it into pieces.

a. לְכָה דוֹדִי can be broken into three parts. The first is about the coming of Shabbat, the second is about the rebuilding of a destroyed Jerusalem and the third goes back to Shabbat. Where does each of these parts begin and end? Shabbat section: Lines 1-10; Jerusalem section: 11-34; Shabbat section: 35-38.

b. Look at the first Shabbat section. What is it about? Verse one is about God being one. It contains the image of "שָׁמוֹר" and "זָכוֹר" being heard at the same time. Verse two is about how Shabbat is older than creation—one of God's earliest gifts.

c. Look at the Jerusalem section. What is it about? It starts with the image of Jerusalem being destroyed, and the singers invite her to "get her act together" because better things are happening.

The poem moves to tell her (Jerusalem) that the messiah is coming. This is told in two images that will be obscure to your students:

1. Son of Jesse refers to David.
2. Through a family that started with Peretz is another reference to David's family and therefore the messiah, who is a descendant of David.

2. Practicing the Hebrew Text ■ [a] INVITE students to work with a partner and practice the prayer. [b] READ or SING the prayers together as a class. [c] INVITE individual students or teams of students to perform individual lines or sections.

לְכָה דוֹדִי

Come, my friend, let's greet the BRIDE	לְכָה דוֹדִי לִקְרַאת כַּלָּה	1.
Let us welcome the face of SHABBAT.	פְּנֵי שַׁבָּת נְקַבְּלָה.	2.
"GUARD" and "REMEMBER" are said as ONE	שָׁמוֹר וְזָכוֹר בְּדִבּוּר אֶחָד	3.
We are able to hear them together because of a UNIFYING God	הִשְׁמִיעָנוּ אֵל הַמְיֻחָד.	4.
ADONAI is ONE and God's NAME is ONE.	יי אֶחָד וּשְׁמוֹ אֶחָד	5.
This all goes to NAME, BEAUTY, and PRAISE.	לְשֵׁם וּלְתִפְאֶרֶת וְלִתְהִלָּה.	6.
To greet SHABBAT let us go	לִקְרַאת שַׁבָּת לְכוּ וְנֵלְכָה	7.
because She is a SOURCE of BLESSING	כִּי הִיא מְקוֹר הַבְּרָכָה.	8.
from the BEGINNING, from BEFORE, She was appointed—	מֵרֹאשׁ מִקֶּדֶם נְסוּכָה	9.
the FINAL CREATION was in the THOUGHT that came First.	סוֹף מַעֲשֶׂה בְּמַחֲשָׁבָה תְּחִלָּה.	10.
Sanctuary of the RULER, RULING city,	מִקְדַּשׁ מֶלֶךְ עִיר מְלוּכָה,	11.
GET Yourself UP, leave your desolation.	קוּמִי צְאִי מִתּוֹךְ הַהֲפֵכָה.	12.
It is too much for You to sit in a valley of tears	רַב לָךְ שֶׁבֶת בְּעֵמֶק הַבָּכָא,	13.
God will act with compassion for You.	וְהוּא יַחֲמוֹל עָלַיִךְ חֶמְלָה.	14.
SHAKE it off. GET UP from the dust.	הִתְנַעֲרִי, מֵעָפָר קוּמִי,	15.
Put on garments of beauty, my people.	לִבְשִׁי בִּגְדֵי תִפְאַרְתֵּךְ עַמִּי.	16.
Soon comes the son of Jesse from Bethlehem—	עַל יַד בֶּן יִשַׁי בֵּית הַלַּחְמִי.	17.
and near to my soul is redemption.	קָרְבָה אֶל נַפְשִׁי גְאָלָהּ.	18.

8

WAKE UP. WAKE UP.	19. הִתְעוֹרְרִי הִתְעוֹרְרִי
because your LIGHT is coming. GET UP and SHINE.	20. כִּי בָא אוֹרֵךְ קוּמִי אוֹרִי.
WAKE. WAKE. Sing my song!	21. עוּרִי עוּרִי שִׁיר דַּבֵּרִי,
ADONAI's honor is revealed in You.	22. כְּבוֹד יי עָלַיִךְ נִגְלָה.
Don't be ashamed. Don't be humiliated.	23. לֹא תֵבשִׁי וְלֹא תִכָּלְמִי,
Why are You down? Why are You depressed?	24. מַה תִּשְׁתּוֹחֲחִי וּמַה תֶּהֱמִי.
You will shelter the poor of my people.	25. בָּךְ יֶחֱסוּ עֲנִיֵּי עַמִּי,
You will be REBUILT out of the RUINS.	26. וְנִבְנְתָה עִיר עַל תִּלָּהּ.
Then Your destroyers will be destroyed	27. וְהָיוּ לִמְשִׁסָּה שֹׁאסָיִךְ
Those who devoured You will be exiled far away.	28. וְרָחֲקוּ כָּל מְבַלְּעָיִךְ.
Your God will REJOICE over You	29. יָשִׂישׂ עָלַיִךְ אֱלֹהָיִךְ
Like a groom REJOICES over a BRIDE.	30. כִּמְשׂושׂ חָתָן עַל כַּלָּה.
Right and left You will SPREAD OUT	31. יָמִין וּשְׂמֹאל תִּפְרֹצִי
And before GOD TREMBLE.	32. וְאֶת יי תַּעֲרִיצִי.
Through a family that started with Peretz (David's family)	33. עַל יַד אִישׁ בֶּן פַּרְצִי,
We shall be glad and happy.	34. וְנִשְׂמְחָה וְנָגִילָה.
Enter in PEACE, Crown of her partner	35. בּוֹאִי בְשָׁלוֹם עֲטֶרֶת בַּעְלָהּ,
With JOY and with GLADNESS	36. גַּם בְּשִׂמְחָה וּבְצָהֳלָה,
In the midst of the BELIEVERS of a TREASURED PEOPLE	37. תּוֹךְ אֱמוּנֵי עַם סְגֻלָּה,
COME BRIDE. COME BRIDE.	38. בּוֹאִי כַלָּה, בּוֹאִי כַלָּה.

9

TRANSLATION/COMMENTARY

This page allows us to translate the chorus to לְכָה דוֹדִי and to talk about the process of preparing for Shabbat.

Big Ideas

1. Growing and reinforcing Hebrew vocabulary leads to a growing affinity with the liturgy.
2. Applying the Hebrew they have to form rough translations of Hebrew prayers (a) helps students to feel closer to those texts, (b) reinforces the Hebrew they are learning and (c) develops a process they can continue to apply to the Siddur.

Learning Activities

1. Introducing/reviewing vocabulary
2. Working out a trial translation
3. Correcting translations
4. Prayer drill

You Know You've Succeeded When...

1. Students work out a reasonable translation of this text.
2. Students correct their translation.

1. Introducing/Reviewing Vocabulary ■ [a] Using VOCABULARY POSTERS and FLASHCARDS, introduce and drill the core vocabulary needed for this translation. [b] Some game playing or team competition is the perfect way to reinforce this vocabulary.

2. Working out a Trial Translation ■ [a] Working in pairs, students should develop their own best TRANSLATION. [b] They should not worry about being perfect—they should worry about coming close. EXPECT a working translation something like:

> **Walk my beloved to greet the bride**
> **face (of) Shabbat we will welcome**

3. Correcting Translations ■

(a) Understand לְכָה as "let us go."

(b) פְּנֵי should be understood as "the face of" or "the presence of"

4. Prayer Drill ■ Practice performing this portion of the prayer. SING or READ it together.

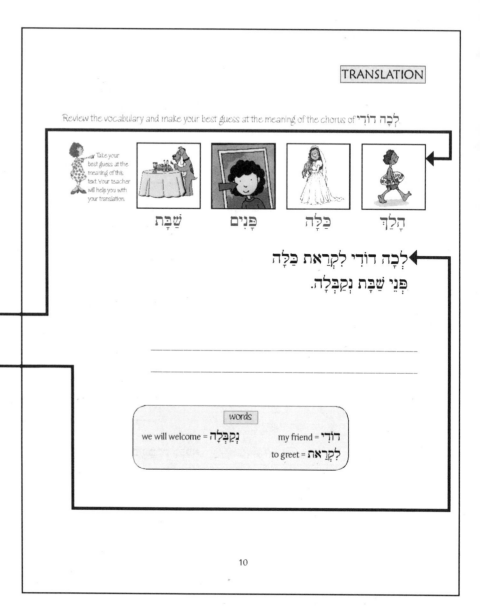

Shabbat Starts with a Sigh

Rabbi Hanokh of Alexander told this story: "When I first became a rabbi this happened in my synagogue. A butcher was working and working. He didn't stop on Friday afternoon to get ready for Shabbat. He kept on chopping and chopping meat. Suddenly, he realized that it might already be Shabbat. He was afraid that he had broken the Torah's rule and been working on the Sabbath. He ran directly to the synagogue. He didn't even take off his bloody apron. He burst through the doors and heard the first words of לְכָה דוֹדִי. He had just made it. He sighed a big sigh of relief. At that moment, the sigh that came out of his mouth was the sigh of all the Jews who were in Egypt. They sighed to God out of their bondage. They, too, stopped their labor when Shabbat came." (Martin Buber, *Tales of the Hasidim, Later Masters*)

Questions

1. How could the sigh of thousands of Jews in Egypt come out of a Polish butcher's mouth?
2. What does this story teach us about the importance of קַבָּלַת שַׁבָּת (welcoming Shabbat)?
3. How can knowing this story help you know where to point your heart when you say לְכָה דוֹדִי?

11

STORY

This page tells a Hasidic story about the process of entering Shabbat. It gives us a window on "welcoming Shabbat."

Big Ideas

- We can relive moments of history in our own lives.
- Shabbat happens better with preparation.
- Shabbat is (in some ways) a state of mind we create.

Learning Activities

1. Read the story.
2. Go over the story in Hevruta.
3. Discuss the questions.

You Know You've Succeeded When...

1. Students can retell the story.
2. Student can provide reasonable answers to the questions.

1. **Read the Story** ■

2. **Go over the Story in Hevruta** ■

3. **Discuss the Questions** ■

   1. **How could the sigh of thousands of Jews in Egypt come out of a Polish butcher's mouth?** *Expect answers like* "He was feeling the same thing that they did." "It was genetically embedded in him." "His situation was similar to theirs."

      You can deepen this by saying something we have been pointing to all year: "We wind up reliving some important Jewish moments in our own lives."

   2. **What does this story teach us about the importance of** קַבָּלַת שַׁבָּת**, welcoming Shabbat?** *Expect answers like* "It is better to prepare for Shabbat." "A person can create a Shabbat way of being." "Shabbat is when we really let go of work— קַבָּלַת שַׁבָּת helps."

      You can deepen this by saying, "Shabbat is partly a state of mind. Getting physically ready is one way of welcoming it. Getting spiritually ready is another. קַבָּלַת שַׁבָּת lets us bring Shabbat into our head and our heart."

   3. **How can knowing this story help you know where to point your heart when you say** לְכָה דוֹדִי**?** *Expect two interesting opposite answers:* (1) We should not be like the butcher and should get ourselves ready for Shabbat. (2) We should be like the butcher and learn to get our heart into Shabbat. We should be able to sigh the way he sighed.

Blank Page

בָּרְכוּ

Lesson 3

This lesson presents the בָּרְכוּ. It introduces the function, theme, language and meaning of the "Call to Worship".

Page 12: We introduce the בָּרְכוּ as the "Call to Worship."

Page 13: We introduce and work with the root ברך, the core word in the בָּרְכוּ.

Page 14: We work out a translation for the בָּרְכוּ and learn its choreography

Page 15: The story of the first time the בָּרְכוּ was said is told. It clues us to focus on the spiritual meaning of this text.

Page 16: The end of the story and questions.

LESSON 3: THE בָּרְכוּ

This page is an overview of the בָּרְכוּ.

Big Ideas

1. The בָּרְכוּ is the way that a community is formed so that worship can proceed.
2. The בָּרְכוּ is a call and response.
3. The בָּרְכוּ is also part of the Torah blessings.

Learning Activities

1. Introducing the unit
2. Exploring the themes
3. Reviewing the key themes

You Know You've Succeeded When...

1. Students can describe the process and purpose of the בָּרְכוּ.
2. Students suggest reasons that the בָּרְכוּ begins the service.

1. Introducing the unit ■ The introduction to the בָּרְכוּ teaches these big concepts:

a. The בָּרְכוּ is the prayer that organizes people into a prayer community. It is the first prayer that requires a מִנְיָן.

b. A מִנְיָן is a quorum of at least ten people. Jewish prayer is a community process.

c. The בָּרְכוּ is a call and response prayer. The leader begins and the group answers. In answering, the group becomes a community.

2. Exploring the Themes ■ Three different Jewish rituals specifically include a call to community as part of their structure. These are the בָּרְכוּ, the blessing before reading Torah, and the z'mun (words of invitation) at the start of Birkat ha-Mazon (Grace after Meals). These rituals suggest two big ideas.

a. Some prayers should not be said alone. They work better with others.

b. To turn a group of people into a prayer community takes a process, a ritual that links them.

3. Reviewing the Key Themes ■

Why do these three events—praying, reading Torah and the end of a meal—require a special way of forming community? There is no single correct answer to this question. But here are some good answers that you and your students can fill in:

• Judaism is a community religion.
• Some things work better when you can share them.
• There are times for solos and times for choirs.
• Some things are scary or hard and work better when you have support.
• These rituals are a way of making people closer.

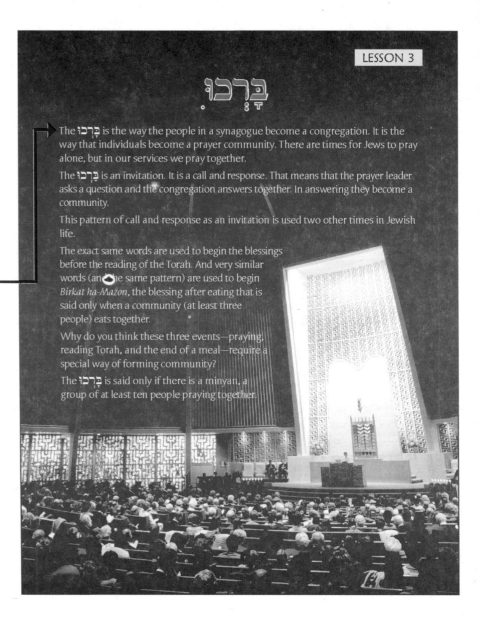

בָּרְכוּ

The בָּרְכוּ is the way the people in a synagogue become a congregation. It is the way that individuals become a prayer community. There are times for Jews to pray alone, but in our services we pray together.

The בָּרְכוּ is an invitation. It is a call and response. That means that the prayer leader asks a question and the congregation answers together. In answering they become a community.

This pattern of call and response as an invitation is used two other times in Jewish life.

The exact same words are used to begin the blessings before the reading of the Torah. And very similar words (and the same pattern) are used to begin Birkat ha-Mazon, the blessing after eating that is said only when a community (at least three people) eats together.

Why do you think these three events—praying, reading Torah, and the end of a meal—require a special way of forming community?

The בָּרְכוּ is said only if there is a minyan, a group of at least ten people praying together.

Can you see the three letters ברך in these words?
It is found in every בְּרָכָה.

ROOT ANALYSIS

בָּרוּךְ ← בָּרְכוּ הַמְבֹרָךְ

blessed = בָּרוּךְ

bless (plural) = בָּרְכוּ

the One Who is blessed = הַמְבֹרָךְ

CLUE: ך = כ ‖ כ = בּ

Practice these words and phrases. Circle all the words that contain the root ברך.

1. בָּרוּךְ כָּבוֹד מְבָרֵךְ מֶלֶךְ מַלְכֵי בָּרָא

2. מְבָרֵךְ שְׁמַע הַמְבֹרָךְ מַלְכֵנוּ בָּרֵךְ בִּרְכַּת

3. בָּרְכוּ אֶת וָעֶד בָּרוּךְ יי הַמְבֹרָךְ לְעוֹלָם

4. בָּרְכוּ אֶת־יי אֶת־יי הַמְבֹרָךְ בָּרְכוּ אֶת־יי הַמְבֹרָךְ

5. בָּרוּךְ יי יי הַמְבֹרָךְ הַמְבֹרָךְ לְעוֹלָם לְעוֹלָם וָעֶד

6. בָּרְכוּ אֶת־יי הַמְבֹרָךְ

7. בָּרוּךְ יי הַמְבֹרָךְ לְעוֹלָם וָעֶד

13

5. Fill in the missing letters of the root ברך ■

• Have students work individually or in pairs to complete the exercise.

ROOT ברך

This page studies the root ברך.

Big Ideas

1. Mastering Hebrew roots dramatically improves comprehension.
2. Looking at words built out of a single root enhances an understanding of Hebrew thinking.

Learning Activities

1. Analysis of the root ברך
2. Identifying words built out of ברך
3. Understanding the icon for the root ברך
4. Reading and identifying activity
5. Filling in the missing letters of the root ברך

You Know You've Succeeded When...

• Students can identify words with the ברך root.

1. Analysis of the Root ברך ■

a. Use the board or flashcards to introduce the root ברך and the words built out of it.

b. Establish the connection between the three words: בָּרוּךְ, בָּרְכוּ and הַמְבֹרָךְ.

c. Remind students about the three forms of the letter כ—בּ, כ and ך.

2. Identifying Words Built out of ברך ■

a. ASK: What word idea connects בָּרוּךְ, בָּרְכוּ and הַמְבֹרָךְ?

b. ESTABLISH that "bless" is the core idea.

3. Understand the Icon for the Root ברך ■

Have students try to make their hands into the same shape as those in the blessing icon. Explain that this is the way the Kohanim (priests) place their hands when they bless the people. You may want to explain that this was done in the Temple and is still done in many Conservative and Orthodox congregations on festivals. It is also done weekly in many synagogues in Israel. [Do you know the Star Trek story about "Spock hands"? If so, you may want to tell this, too.]

4. Reading and Identifying Activity ■

a. Let students prepare these lines with a *hevruta* partner.

b. Go over the passage. Invite individual students to read. Ask the entire class to read out together the words built out of the root ברך.

TRANSLATION/COMMENTARY

This page has students work on a translation of בָּרְכוּ and look at a commentary on the שְׁמַע at Mt. Sinai.

Big Ideas

1. Growing and reinforcing Hebrew vocabulary leads to a growing affinity with the liturgy.
2. Applying the Hebrew they have to form rough translations of Hebrew prayers (a) helps students to feel closer to those texts, (b) reinforces the Hebrew they are learning and (c) develops a process they can continue to apply to the Siddur.
3. Choreography of the בָּרְכוּ.

Learning Activities

1. Introducing/reviewing vocabulary
2. Working out a trial translation
3. Correcting translations
4. Prayer drill
5. Discussing commentary

You Know You've Succeeded When...

1. Students work out a reasonable translation of this text.
2. Students correct their translation.
3. Students unpack the choreography of the בָּרְכוּ.

1. Introducing/Reviewing Vocabulary ■ [a] Using VOCABULARY POSTERS and FLASHCARDS, introduce and drill the core vocabulary needed for this translation. [b] Some game playing or team competition is the perfect way to reinforce this vocabulary.

2. Working out a Trial Translation ■ [a] Working in pairs, students should develop their own best TRANSLATION. [b] They should not worry about being perfect—they should worry about coming close. EXPECT a working translation something like:

Bless God the Blessed
Bless God the Blessed to the World and more.

3. Correcting Translations ■

[הַמְבֹרָךְ]. This means "The One Who is Blessed."

לְעוֹלָם וָעֶד is very much like the *Toy Story* character Buzz Lightyear's "To infinity and beyond." The trick here is understanding that "עוֹלָם" means both "the world" and "all of reality" (like the whole cosmos) or "eternity". The idea here is that "the world" was the largest concept that ancient people could think of when it came to talking about how Hebrew evolved. וָעֶד means "and more." That explains how "to the world and more" comes out as "forever and ever."

4. Prayer Drill ■ Practice performing this portion of the prayer. SING or READ it together.

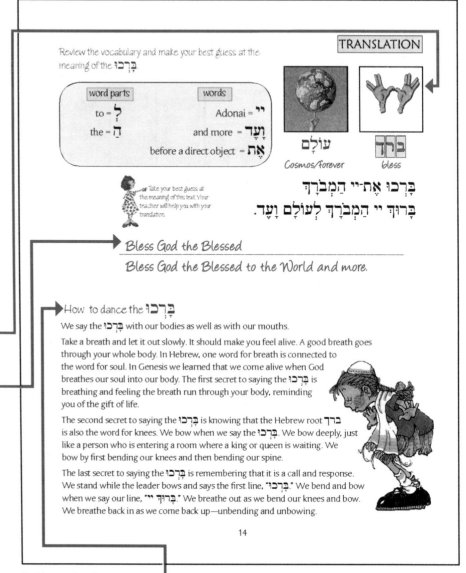

Review the vocabulary and make your best guess at the meaning of the בָּרְכוּ.

word parts	words
to = לְ	Adonai = יי
the = הַ	and more = וָעֶד
	before a direct object = אֶת

עוֹלָם — Cosmos/forever

ברך — bless

Take your best guess at the meaning of this text. Your teacher will help you with your translation.

בָּרְכוּ אֶת־יי הַמְבֹרָךְ
בָּרוּךְ יי הַמְבֹרָךְ לְעוֹלָם וָעֶד.

Bless God the Blessed

Bless God the Blessed to the World and more.

How to dance the בָּרְכוּ

We say the בָּרְכוּ with our bodies as well as with our mouths.

Take a breath and let it out slowly. It should make you feel alive. A good breath goes through your whole body. In Hebrew, one word for breath is connected to the word for soul. In Genesis we learned that we come alive when God breathes our soul into our body. The first secret to saying the בָּרְכוּ is breathing and feeling the breath run through your body, reminding you of the gift of life.

The second secret to saying the בָּרְכוּ is knowing that the Hebrew root ברך is also the word for knees. We bow when we say the בָּרְכוּ. We bow deeply, just like a person who is entering a room where a king or queen is waiting. We bow by first bending our knees and then bending our spine.

The last secret to saying the בָּרְכוּ is remembering that it is a call and response. We stand while the leader bows and says the first line, "בָּרְכוּ." We bend and bow when we say our line, "יי בָּרוּךְ." We breathe out as we bend our knees and bow. We breathe back in as we come back up—unbending and unbowing.

14

5. Discussing Commentary ■ READ and DISCUSS "How to Dance the בָּרְכוּ."

Read the text aloud as the students stand-up and do the movements and the breathing. Ask, "How does standing or bowing or lifting up onto your toes help you to get into the right spirit for prayer?" There are no correct answers to this question. The bottom line here is that we just know that it does.

The Power of a Minyan

The Midrash teaches that Abraham figured out that ten was the smallest number of people to make sure that prayers had a good chance of convincing God. Abraham realized this when he was trying to save Sodom. He argued with God that it was wrong to destroy Sodom if enough righteous people lived there. God agreed not to destroy the city if there were fifty good people. Then Abraham tried smaller numbers and stopped at ten. We've used ten ever since. Ten or more Jews praying together are a minyan. The Hasidim understood the power of a minyan and told this story.

There was a blind rebbe who was called the Seer of Lublin. The Seer could not see things through his eyes but he saw in other ways. One of the students of the Seer was a man who lived in a town where there were no other Jews. One week a year the student would leave his farm, ride almost two days on his horse, and then spend a week studying with, praying with, and being part of the Seer's community.

Once he rode into Lublin late on a Thursday afternoon. He went to put his horse away in the stable and found the Seer waiting for him. Almost magically, the blind Seer called him by name and said, "Go home."

15

STORY: THE POWER OF A MINYAN

This story combines a midrash about Abraham with a traditional Hasidic story.

Big Ideas

- The מִנְיָן becomes the minimum number needed to save the world. That makes a מִנְיָן a "world-saving" team.
- The מִנְיָן becomes a source of strength for the individual who is a member of that group.
- When we gather as a מִנְיָן we are joining together for strength greater than our own indivudual strength alone.
- A מִנְיָן can sometimes accomplish some things that an individual cannot.

Learning Activities

1. Read the Story
2. Go over the story in Hevruta.
3. Discuss the Questions

You Know You've Succeeded When...

1. Students can retell the story.
2. Student can provide reasonable answers to the questions.

1. Read the story ■

2. Go over the story in Hevruta ■ Continued on next page.

3. Discuss the questions ■

1. **What do you think this story means?** Meaning is subjective. Different students will hear different meanings. Enjoy them all. Some may include: Prayer can heal. People can make a difference. Rabbis don't always know best, etc. If it is not stated, make sure that you add: "There is something powerful in being part of a community—especially a prayer community."

2. **Why is ten the right number for a מִנְיָן?** (We have discussed this on the page 40.) It is rooted in the two midrashim, one about Noah's family and one about Lot's family. The core idea is that ten seems to be a minimum number to form a community. Students may express this in may ways—and getting to an exact answer here is not important.

3. **How does a מִנְיָן work miracles?** No one knows the answer to this question. Some guesses may include: More people are heard by God better than a single individual. People in the מִנְיָן take care of each other. When you are part of a מִנְיָן you get the support to be at your best (like basketball players do from the crowd), etc. More than finding the "right answer," you want to discuss: "Does it seem possible to you that a מִנְיָן can work miracles?"

4. **How can this story help you know where to point your heart when you say the בָּרְכוּ?** There will be many ways of answering this, but the discussion should include: (1) that when we say the בָּרְכוּ we become part of a prayer community; (2) that there is a power that can be found in a community; (3) that we help others and others help us; and so on.

The man said, "But—"

The Seer said, "Go home and get there before Shabbat starts."

The man said, "But it is Thursday afternoon, and my farm is two days away."

The Seer said, "Go," and the man had no choice. He got on his tired horse and rode through the night.

Near morning he came to an inn. The man said, "I am tired. My horse is tired We will stop for food and water and then we will rush on." In the inn were nine other Jews. They begged the man to stay with them and be the tenth person in their minyan for Shabbat. He explained that the Seer had told him to go home, and he said, "Sorry, but no."

The man ate and drank, but fell asleep and woke just before Shabbat. He panicked when he realized that he was stuck. He became the tenth in their minyan.

It was an amazing Shabbat. When the group sang together it was as if angels were singing with them. When they danced together, it was as if they were dancing in the air. When they studied together, walls of fire surrounded them.

As soon as Shabbat was over, the man got back on his horse and rode through the night to get back to Lublin to apologize. When he got there the Seer was waiting. The Seer called him by name, and said, "You were supposed to die this Shabbat. That is why I wanted you to return home."

The man said, "I am still alive."

The Seer explained, "Sometimes a minyan has more power than a miracle-working rebbe." *From Martin Buber's Tales of the Hasidim*

> Questions
> 1. What do you think this story means?
> 2. Why is ten the right number for a minyan?
> 3. How does a minyan work miracles?
> 4. How can this story help you know where to point your heart when you say the בָּרְכוּ?

16

מַעֲרִיב עֲרָבִים

Lesson 4

Blank Page

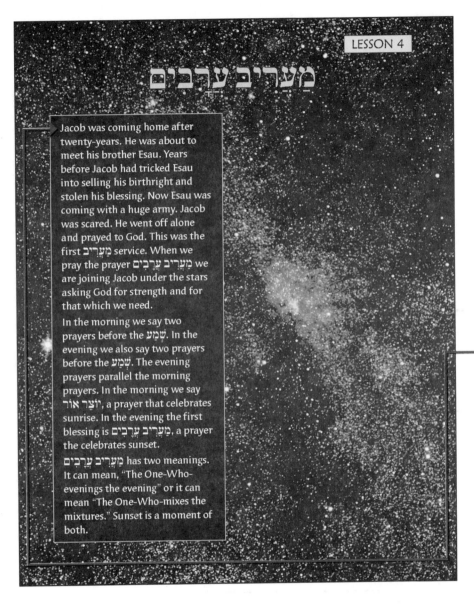

מַעֲרִיב עֲרָבִים

Jacob was coming home after twenty-years. He was about to meet his brother Esau. Years before Jacob had tricked Esau into selling his birthright and stolen his blessing. Now Esau was coming with a huge army. Jacob was scared. He went off alone and prayed to God. This was the first מַעֲרִיב service. When we pray the prayer מַעֲרִיב עֲרָבִים we are joining Jacob under the stars asking God for strength and for that which we need.

In the morning we say two prayers before the שְׁמַע. In the evening we also say two prayers before the שְׁמַע. The evening prayers parallel the morning prayers. In the morning we say יוֹצֵר אוֹר, a prayer that celebrates sunrise. In the evening the first blessing is מַעֲרִיב עֲרָבִים, a prayer the celebrates sunset.

מַעֲרִיב עֲרָבִים has two meanings. It can mean, "The One-Who-evenings the evening" or it can mean "The One-Who-mixes the mixtures." Sunset is a moment of both.

LESSON 4: The מַעֲרִיב עֲרָבִים

This page is an overview of the מַעֲרִיב עֲרָבִים.

Big Ideas

1. מַעֲרִיב עֲרָבִים has a midrashic origin in Jacob's asking God for help.
2. מַעֲרִיב עֲרָבִים fills the slot of the first בְּרָכָה before the שְׁמַע in the evening service.
3. מַעֲרִיב עֲרָבִים has two meanings, "brings on the evening" and "mixes the mixtures."

Learning Activities

1. Introducing the unit
2. Exploring the themes
3. Reviewing the key themes

You Know You've Succeeded When...

1. Students can describe the midrashic origins of the מַעֲרִיב עֲרָבִים as starting with Jacob.
2. Students can state the place of מַעֲרִיב עֲרָבִים in the structure of the evening Shema and her בְּרָכוֹת.
3. Students can state the two different meanings for the phrase מַעֲרִיב עֲרָבִים.

1. **Introducing the Unit** ■ If your students have previously studied the morning service, compare מַעֲרִיב עֲרָבִים to יוֹצֵר אוֹר. Turn to page 18 and look at English translation of מַעֲרִיב עֲרָבִים. Establish that its themes are evening and creation.

2. **Exploring the Themes** ■ Read the text. Go over the three big ideas. Each is expressed in one of the paragraphs:

   a. Jacob is connected to the מַעֲרִיב service and the מַעֲרִיב prayer.

   b. There are two בְּרָכוֹת before the שְׁמַע in the evening service and two afterwards. The first slot is a "creation בְּרָכָה" slot that is taken by מַעֲרִיב עֲרָבִים.

   c. מַעֲרִיב עֲרָבִים has two meanings, "Who brings on the evening," and "Who mixes the mixtures." These offer two different views of evening—one as a distinct new reality, the other as a mixture of day and night.

3. **Reviewing Key Themes** ■

   1. The מַעֲרִיב service and the מַעֲרִיב prayer are connected to Jacob.

   2. מַעֲרִיב עֲרָבִים is the first בְּרָכָה before the שְׁמַע. It talks about creation.

   3. מַעֲרִיב עֲרָבִים has two meanings, "Who brings on the evening," and "Who mixes the mixtures."

TEXT/TRANSLATION/COMMENTARY

This page contains the Hebrew and English text of the מַעֲרִיב עֲרָבִים.

Big Ideas

1. When we enable students to perfect performances of core liturgy we make it possible for them to far more easily participate in communal worship.

2. By scanning the English of prayers students can grow insights into the meaning of the liturgy.

3. The Torah service and eating are similar spiritual practices.

Learning Activities

1. Scanning the English text
2. Practicing the Hebrew text

You Know You've Succeeded When...

1 Students describe insights gained from looking at the English text.
2. Students practice their performance of the Hebrew text.

1. Scanning the English Text ■ INVITE students to SCAN the English translation of these prayers. ASK them what "big ideas" they can find by looking.

INSIGHT that might be shared: This prayer teaches that new things are continually being created and old things are continually being recreated. Creation is ongoing. This is a wonderful chance for a discussion of how something "old" can seem "new" at a given moment.

2. Practicing the Hebrew Text ■ [a] INVITE students to work with a partner and practice the prayer. [b] READ or SING the prayers together as a class. [c] INVITE individual students or teams of students to perform individual lines or sections.

מַעֲרִיב עֲרָבִים

1.	BLESSED are You, ADONAI	בָּרוּךְ אַתָּה יי
2.	our God, RULER of the COSMOS	אֱלֹהֵינוּ מֶלֶךְ הָעוֹלָם
3.	The ONE Who by WORD	אֲשֶׁר בִּדְבָרוֹ
4.	MIXES the mixtures (and EVENINGS the evening).	מַעֲרִיב עֲרָבִים
5.	The ONE Who with WISDOM OPENS the GATES	בְּחָכְמָה פּוֹתֵחַ שְׁעָרִים
6.	with UNDERSTANDING CHANGES the TIMES	וּבִתְבוּנָה מְשַׁנֶּה עִתִּים
7.	and SWITCHES the SEASONS	וּמַחֲלִיף אֶת הַזְּמַנִּים
8.	and ORDERS the stars	וּמְסַדֵּר אֶת הַכּוֹכָבִים
9.	in their heavenly ORBITS according to plan.	בְּמִשְׁמְרוֹתֵיהֶם בָּרָקִיעַ כִּרְצוֹנוֹ.
10.	CREATOR of day and night.	בּוֹרֵא יוֹם וָלַיְלָה
11.	The ONE Who ROLLS light into darkness	גּוֹלֵל אוֹר מִפְּנֵי חֹשֶׁךְ
12.	and darkness into light.	וְחֹשֶׁךְ מִפְּנֵי אוֹר.
13.	The One Who MAKES day pass and BRINGS on evening	וּמַעֲבִיר יוֹם וּמֵבִיא לָיְלָה
14.	And the ONE Who DIVIDES between day and between night.	וּמַבְדִּיל בֵּין יוֹם וּבֵין לָיְלָה
15.	This One's name is ADONAI TZVA'OT (ADONAI, The Warrior Against Evil).	יי צְבָאוֹת שְׁמוֹ.
16.	God—The ONE Who is life and continuity	אֵל חַי וְקַיָּם
17.	Please, always ruler over us	תָּמִיד יִמְלֹךְ עָלֵינוּ
18.	forever and always.	לְעוֹלָם וָעֶד.
19.	BLESSED are You, ADONAI,	בָּרוּךְ אַתָּה יי
20.	The ONE Who MIXES the mixtures (and EVENINGS the evening).	הַמַּעֲרִיב עֲרָבִים.

18

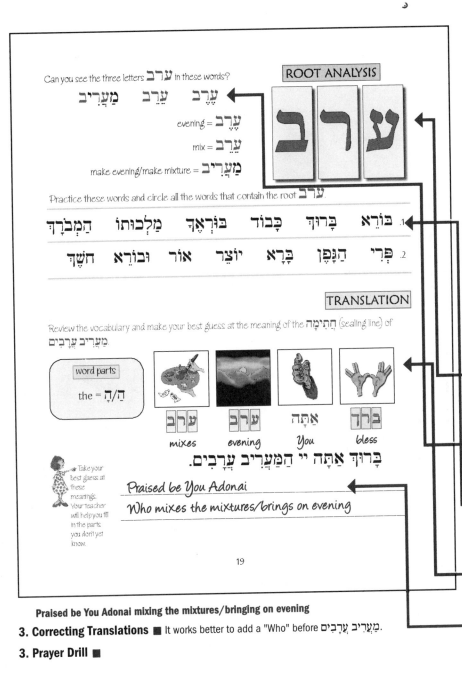

Left workbook page (reproduced):

Can you see the three letters עָרָב in these words?

ROOT ANALYSIS

עָרָב   עֶרֶב   מַעֲרִיב

evening = עֶרֶב

mix = עָרַב

make evening/make mixture = מַעֲרִיב

Practice these words and circle all the words that contain the root עָרָב.

1. בּוֹרֵא   בָּרוּךְ   כָּבוֹד   בּוֹרְאֲךָ   מַלְכוּתוֹ   הַמְבֹרָךְ

2. פְּרִי   הַגֶּפֶן   בָּרָא   יוֹצֵר   אוֹר   וּבוֹרֵא   חֹשֶׁךְ

TRANSLATION

Review the vocabulary and make your best guess at the meaning of the חֲתִימָה (sealing line) of מַעֲרִיב עֲרָבִים.

word parts

the = הַ/הָ

mixes   evening   You   bless

בָּרוּךְ אַתָּה יי הַמַּעֲרִיב עֲרָבִים.

Praised be You Adonai
Who mixes the mixtures/brings on evening

Take your best guess at these meanings. Your teacher will help you fill in the parts you don't yet know.

19

ROOT עָרָב AND TRANSLATION

This page begins the study of roots by unpacking the root עָרָב, and the translation of the first part of the בְּרָכָה.

Big Ideas

1. Mastering Hebrew roots dramatically improves comprehension.
2. Looking at words built out of a single root enhances an understanding of Hebrew thinking.
3. Growing and reinforcing Hebrew vocabulary leads to an affinity with the liturgy.
4. Applying the Hebrew they have to form rough translations of Hebrew prayers (a) helps students to feel closer to those texts, (b) reinforces the Hebrew they are learning and (c) develops a process they can continue to apply to the Siddur.

Learning Activities

1. Analysis of the root עָרָב
2. Identifying words built out of עָרָב
3. Reading and identifying activity
4. Introducing/reviewing vocabulary
5. Working out a trial translation
6. Correcting translations
7. Prayer drill

You Know You've Succeeded When...

1. Students can identify words with a עָרָב root.
2. Students work out a reasonable translation of this text.
3. Students correct their translation.

1. Analysis of the Root עָרָב ■

a. Use the board or flashcards to introduce the root עָרָב and the words built out of it.

b. Establish the connection between the three words מַעֲרִיב, עֶרֶב, עָרַב. NOTE: "evening" and "mixing" are the core idea.

2. Identifying Words Built out of עָרָב ■

a. ASK: What word idea connects מַעֲרִיב, עֶרֶב, עָרַב?

b. ESTABLISH that these are the same words with differing tenses.

3. Reading and Identifying Activity ■

a. Let students prepare these lines with a *Hevruta* partner.

b. Go over the passage. Invite individual students to read. Ask the entire class to read out together the words built out of the root עָרָב.

> עָרָב words are missing from this exercise. This will be corrected in reprints.

4. Introducing/Reviewing Vocabulary ■

[a] Using VOCABULARY POSTERS and FLASHCARDS, introduce and drill the core vocabulary needed for this translation. [b] Some game playing or team competition is the perfect way to reinforce this vocabulary.

5. Working out a Trial Translation ■

[a] Working in pairs, students should develop their own best TRANSLATION. [b] They should not worry about being perfect. EXPECT a working translation something like:

Praised be You Adonai mixing the mixtures/bringing on evening

3. Correcting Translations ■

It works better to add a "Who" before מַעֲרִיב עֲרָבִים.

3. Prayer Drill ■

TRANSLATION/COMMENTARY

This page has students work on a translation of a second part of מַעֲרִיב עֲרָבִים and talk about sunsets.

Big Ideas

1. Growing and reinforcing Hebrew vocabulary leads to a growing affinity with the liturgy.
2. Applying the Hebrew they have to form rough translations of Hebrew prayers (a) helps students to feel closer to those texts, (b) reinforces the Hebrew they are learning and (c) develops a process they can continue to apply to the Siddur.

Learning Activities

1. Introducing/reviewing vocabulary
2. Working out a trial translation
3. Correcting translations
4. Prayer drill
5. Discussing commentary

You Know You've Succeeded When...

1. Students work out a reasonable translation of this text.
2. Students correct their translation.
3. Students unpack the choreography of the מַעֲרִיב עֲרָבִים.

1. Introducing/Reviewing Vocabulary ■ [a] Using VOCABULARY POSTERS and FLASHCARDS, introduce and drill the core vocabulary needed for this translation. [b] Some game playing or team competition is the perfect way to reinforce this vocabulary.

2. Working out a Trial Translation ■ [a] Working in pairs, students should develop their own best TRANSLATION. [b] They should not worry about being perfect—they should worry about coming close. EXPECT a working translation something like:
Rolls light in the face of darkness and darkness in the face of light.

3. Correcting Translations ■

מִפְּנֵי means "from before."

4. Prayer Drill ■ Practice performing this portion of the prayer. SING or READ it together.

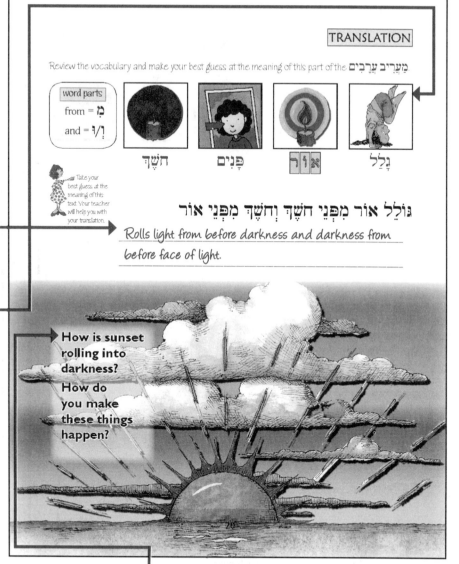

TRANSLATION

Review the vocabulary and make your best guess at the meaning of this part of the מַעֲרִיב עֲרָבִים

word parts
from = מ
and = וְ/וּ

חֹשֶׁךְ   פָּנִים   אוֹר   גָּלַל

Take your best guess at the meaning of this text. Your teacher will help you with your translation.

גּוֹלֵל אוֹר מִפְּנֵי חֹשֶׁךְ וְחֹשֶׁךְ מִפְּנֵי אוֹר

Rolls light from before darkness and darkness from before face of light.

How is sunset rolling into darkness?

How do you make these things happen?

5. Discussing Commentary ■ Read and discuss the questions. "How is sunset rolling into darkness?" and "How do you make these things happen?" should elicit personal answers.

It Happened in the Middle of the Night

At the Passover Seder the first song that we sing after the formal service is over, just before דַיֵּנוּ *Dayeinu*, says, "It happened in the middle of the night." This is from a teaching that the Exodus from Egypt began at night. When we remember that the Jews were liberated from Egypt we remember that many important Jewish events happened at night. We learned that God saved Abraham from both Avimelekh and Laban at night. We learn that Jacob escaped his wrestling match with the angel at night. The Israelites defeated the Canaanite army of Sisera at night. Nebuchadnezzar was defeated at night and Daniel was rescued at night. Haman was stopped and defeated at night, too. And the Messiah will come at night as well. Night is the time of redemption. It is when we are saved.

Usually we are scared of the darkness because it is a time of no light. Usually we think of the night as a bad time, but the Midrash says that good things happen at night. It says, "Rome was connected to the sun, Israel to the moon. During the day the sun wipes out the moon, but at night it can shine. When Rome sets, Israel has a chance to shine." In our life, there are many bright and loud things that hide other things. Night time teaches us that God has "a still small voice" and a hidden light. Night is a time when we can connect to God. *(Genesis Rabbah 6.3)*

Questions

1. What is so special about the night?
2. In ancient times Rome was a huge empire that conquered Israel and kept us from practicing our own religion. The Roman Empire was huge and lasted a long time. What is like the Roman Empire today?
3. How can knowing this story help you to point your heart when you say the prayer מַעֲרִיב עֲרָבִים?

21

STORY

The midrash explains that nighttime comes with its own opportunities to feel close to God.

Big Ideas

1. Nighttime was the time of many redemptions for the Jewish people.
2. Sun stands for Rome. The moon stands for Jacob.
3. Nighttime offers its own special connection to God.

Learning Activities

1. Read the story
2. Go over the story in Hevruta.
3. Discuss the questions

You Know You've Succeeded When...

1. Students can retell the elements.
2. Student can provide reasonable answers to the questions.

1. Read the Story ■

2. Go over the Story in Hevruta ■

3. Discuss the Questions ■

1. **What is so special about the night?** The night is a special spiritual time recalling many redemptions in the past and giving us a quiet alone time to connect to God.

2. **In ancient times, Rome was a huge empire that conquered Israel and kept us from practicing our own religion. The Roman Empire was huge and lasted a long time. What is like the Roman Empire today?** This question calls for personal association. Expect such answers as "terrorism," "Western culture" and other contemporary evils.

3. **How can knowing this story help you to point your heart when you say the prayer מַעֲרִיב עֲרָבִים?** It gets us into a nighttime groove. It gets us ready to feel the spirituality of nighttime.

Blank Page

אַהֲבַת עוֹלָם

Lesson 5

Page 22: An introduction to אַהֲבַת עוֹלָם, rooting the prayer in Jeremiah's teaching and establishing its position as the second בְּרָכָה before the שְׁמַע in the evening service.

Page 23: A text and translation of אַהֲבַת עוֹלָם.

Page 24: The root חיה and a translation of כִּי הֵם חַיֵּינוּ are explored.

Lesson 6

Page 25: The root אהב is explored.

Page 26: The final line, בָּרוּךְ אַתָּה יי אוֹהֵב עַמּוֹ יִשְׂרָאֵל, is translated, and the story of Rabbi Akiva and Rachel is begun.

Page 27: The story of Rabbi Akiva and Rachel is completed.

LESSON 5: אַהֲבַת עוֹלָם

This is the second בְּרָכָה before the שְׁמַע.

Big Ideas

1. The image of אַהֲבַת עוֹלָם "eternal love" comes from the prophet Jeremiah.
2. אַהֲבַת עוֹלָם is the second בְּרָכָה before the שְׁמַע in the evening.
3. The giving of the Torah was a huge act of love.

Learning Activities

1. Introducing the unit
2. Exploring the themes
3. Reviewing the key themes

You Know You've Succeeded When...

1. Students can describe the origins of the phrase אַהֲבַת עוֹלָם.
2. Students can locate the אַהֲבַת עוֹלָם in the structure of the service.

1. Introducing the Unit ■ Look at the English translation of אַהֲבַת עוֹלָם on page 23. Establish that the theme of this prayer is the giving of the Torah as an act of love.

2. Exploring the Themes ■ CONVEY THE INFORMATION IN THE INTRODUCTION: [a] The image of אַהֲבַת עוֹלָם, "eternal love," comes from the prophet Jeremiah, [b] the location of אַהֲבַת עוֹלָם is aas the second בְּרָכָה before the שְׁמַע in the evening service and [c] the giving of the Torah was a huge act of love.

3. Reviewing the Key Themes ■

1. The image of אַהֲבַת עוֹלָם "eternal love" comes from the prophet Jeremiah.
2. אַהֲבַת עוֹלָם is the second בְּרָכָה before the שְׁמַע in the evening.
3. The giving of the Torah was a huge act of love.

LESSON 5

אַהֲבַת עוֹלָם

Jeremiah was a prophet who gave two messages. First, he told Israel that God would destroy their country if they didn't go back to following the Torah. Then, when Babylonia destroyed Israel, he gave them a message of comfort. He told them that God still loved them. One of the things he said was, "The Eternal appeared to me in the distance, saying, 'Yes, I have loved you with an everlasting love, therefore with lovingkindness have I drawn you'" (Jeremiah 31.1-3). Even when God seems far away—we are still loved.

אַהֲבַת עוֹלָם is the second blessing before the שְׁמַע in the evening. It is a parallel to אַהֲבָה רַבָּה that is the second blessing before the שְׁמַע in the morning. It begins with Jeremiah's teaching of "everlasting love." This prayer teaches that the giving of Torah was a huge act of love. Torah teaches us good ways of living and helps us know who we are. Torah also helps us get close to God.

אַהֲבַת עוֹלָם

1. אַהֲבַת עוֹלָם	With Cosmic LOVE FOREVER
2. בֵּית יִשְׂרָאֵל עַמְּךָ אָהַבְתָּ.	You LOVED Your People, the Families of Israel.
3. תּוֹרָה וּמִצְוֹת חֻקִּים וּמִשְׁפָּטִים	Torah and Mitzvot, Hukkim and Mishpatim
4. אוֹתָנוּ לִמַּדְתָּ.	You have taught us.
5. עַל כֵּן יי אֱלֹהֵינוּ	Because of this, Adonai, our God,
6. בְּשָׁכְבֵנוּ וּבְקוּמֵנוּ	when we LIE DOWN and when we GET UP
7. נָשִׂיחַ בְּחֻקֶּיךָ	we will talk about Your Hukkim
8. וְנִשְׂמַח בְּדִבְרֵי תוֹרָתֶךָ	and celebrate the WORDS of Your Torah
9. וּבְמִצְוֹתֶיךָ	and in Your MITZVOT
10. לְעוֹלָם וָעֶד.	FOREVER and ALWAYS.
11. כִּי הֵם חַיֵּינוּ	Because—They insure our LIVES
12. וְאֹרֶךְ יָמֵינוּ	and they extend our DAYS
13. וּבָהֶם נֶהְגֶּה יוֹמָם וָלָיְלָה.	and about them we will THINK DAY and NIGHT.
14. וְאַהֲבָתְךָ אַל תָּסִיר מִמֶּנּוּ	Please: never take Your LOVE away from us
15. לְעוֹלָמִים.	not EVEN EVER.
16. בָּרוּךְ אַתָּה יי	BLESSED are You, ADONAI,
17. אוֹהֵב עַמּוֹ יִשְׂרָאֵל.	The ONE Who LOVES Israel.

23

TEXT, TRANSLATION & COMMENTARY

This page contains the Hebrew and English text of אַהֲבַת עוֹלָם. It should be used for both introducing the prayer and perfecting its performance.

Big Ideas

1. When we enable students to perfect performances of core liturgy we make it possible for them to far more easily participate in communal worship.

2. By scanning the English of prayers students can grow insights into the meaning of the liturgy.

Learning Activities

1. Scanning the English text
2. Practicing the Hebrew text

You Know You've Succeeded When...

1. Students describe insights gained from looking at the English text.
2. Students practice their performance of the Hebrew text.
3. Students read, discuss and respond to the commentary.

1. Scanning the English Text ■ INVITE students to SCAN the English translation of these prayers. ASK them what "big ideas" they can find by looking. INSIGHTS that might be shared include:

a. God loves Israel.
b. Because of Your love we center our lives in Torah and mitzvot.
c. In turn they shape our lives.

2. Practicing the Hebrew Text ■ [a] INVITE students to work with a partner and practice the prayer. [b] READ or SING the prayers together as a class. [c] INVITE individual students or teams of students to perform individual lines or sections.

ROOT חי AND TRANSLATION

This page begins the study of roots by unpacking the root חי and the translation of the first part of the בְּרָכָה.

Big Ideas

1. Mastering Hebrew roots dramatically improves comprehension.
2. Looking at words built out of a single root enhances an understanding of Hebrew thinking.
4. Growing and reinforcing Hebrew vocabulary leads to an affinity with the liturgy.
5. Applying the Hebrew they have to form rough translations of Hebrew prayers (a) helps students to feel closer to those texts, (b) reinforces the Hebrew they are learning and (c) develops a process they can continue to apply to the Siddur.

Learning Activities

1. Analysis of the root חי
2. Identifying words built out of חי
3. Reading and identifying activity
4. Introducing/reviewing vocabulary
5. Working out a trial translation
6. Correcting translations
7. Prayer drill

You Know You've Succeeded When...

1. Students can identify words with a ערב root.
2. Students work out a reasonable translation of this text.
3. Students correct their translation.

1. Analysis of the Root חיה ■
a. Use the board or flashcards to introduce the root חי and the words built out of it.
b. Establish the connection between the three words: חַיֵּינוּ, לְחַיִּים, חַי.

2. Identifying Words Built out of חיה ■
a. ASK: What word idea connects חַיֵּינוּ, לְחַיִּים, חַי?
b. Have students explain how the core meaning "life/live" is part of each word.

3. Reading and Identifying Activity ■
a. Let students prepare these lines with a Hevruta partner.
b. Go over the passage. Invite individual students to read. Ask the entire class to read out together the words built out of the root חי.

4. Introducing/Reviewing Vocabulary ■ [a] Using VOCABULARY POSTERS and FLASHCARDS, introduce and drill the core vocabulary needed for this translation. [b] Some game playing or team competition is the perfect way to reinforce this vocabulary.

5. Working out a Trial Translation ■ [a] Working in pairs, students should develop their own best TRANSLATION. [b] They should not worry about being perfect. EXPECT a working translation something like:

Because these are our lives and the length of our days and in them drive day and night.

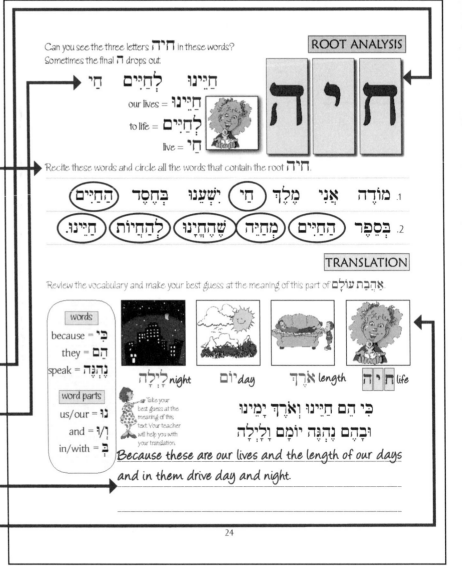

6. Correcting Translations ■
- מַלְכוּת means "kingdom" rather than "king";
- עוֹלָם means "eternity" rather than "world".

7. Prayer Drill ■

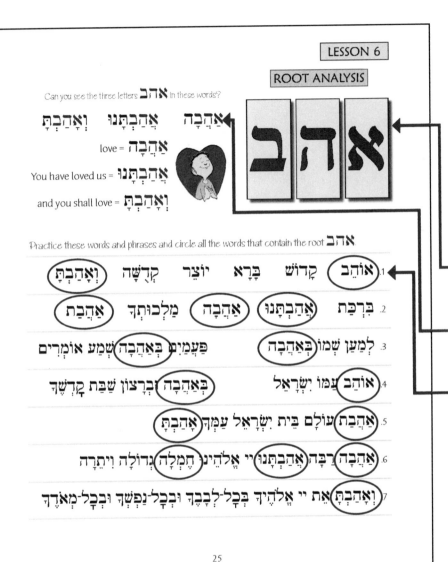

LESSON 6

ROOT ANALYSIS

Can you see the three letters אהב in these words?

אֲהַבְתָּנוּ   וְאָהַבְתָּ   אַהֲבָה

love = אַהֲבָה

You have loved us = אֲהַבְתָּנוּ

and you shall love = וְאָהַבְתָּ

Practice these words and phrases and circle all the words that contain the root אהב.

1. (אוֹהֵב) קָדוֹשׁ בָּרָא יוֹצֵר קְדֻשָּׁה (וְאָהַבְתָּ)

2. בִּרְכַּת (אַהֲבַת) (אֲהַבְתָּנוּ) (אַהֲבָה) מַלְכוּתְךָ

3. לְמַעַן שְׁמוֹ (בְּאַהֲבָה) פְּעָמִים שְׁמַע אוֹמְרִים

4. (בְּאַהֲבָה) אוֹהֵב עַמּוֹ יִשְׂרָאֵל בְּרָצוֹן שַׁבַּת קָדְשֶׁךָ

5. (אַהֲבַת) עוֹלָם בֵּית יִשְׂרָאֵל עַמְּךָ (אָהַבְתָּ)

6. (אַהֲבָה) (רַבָּה) (אֲהַבְתָּנוּ) יְיָ אֱלֹהֵינוּ חֶמְלָה גְדוֹלָה וִיתֵרָה

7. (וְאָהַבְתָּ) אֵת יְיָ אֱלֹהֶיךָ בְּכָל־לְבָבְךָ וּבְכָל־נַפְשְׁךָ וּבְכָל־מְאֹדֶךָ

25

LESSON 6: ROOTS אהב

This page studies the root אהב.

Big Ideas

1. Mastering Hebrew roots dramatically improves comprehension.
2. Looking at words built out of a single root enhances an understanding of Hebrew thinking.

Learning Activities

1. Analysis of the root אהב
2. Identifying words built out of אהב
3. Reading and identifying activity

You Know You've Succeeded When...

• Students can identify words with the אהב root.

1. Analysis of the Root אהב

a. Use the board or flashcards to introduce the root אהב and the words built out of it.

b. Establish the connection between the three words: וְאָהַבְתָּ, אֲהַבְתָּנוּ, אַהֲבָה.

2. Identifying Words Built out of אהב

a. ASK: What word idea connects וְאָהַבְתָּ, אֲהַבְתָּנוּ, אַהֲבָה?

b. Have students explain how the core meaning "love" is part of each word.

3. Reading and Identifying Activity

a. Let students prepare these lines with a *Hevruta* partner.

b. Go over the passage. Invite individual students to read. Ask the entire class to read out together the words built out of the root אהב.

c. Use this exercise for extra practice. For an additional challenge, name the source of the last three lines.

Line 5: אַהֲבַת עוֹלָם

Line 6: אַהֲבָה רַבָּה

Line 7: וְאָהַבְתָּ (שְׁמַע).

TRANSLATION AND STORY

On this page we are going to construct a translation of the חֲתִימָה for אַהֲבַת עוֹלָם and begin the story *Rabbi Akiva and Rachel*.

Big Ideas

1. Growing and reinforcing Hebrew vocabulary leads to a growing affinity with the liturgy.

2. Applying the Hebrew they have to form rough translations of Hebrew prayers (a) helps students to feel closer to those texts, (b) reinforces the Hebrew they are learning, and (c) develops a process they can continue to apply to the Siddur.

Learning Activities

1. Introducing/reviewing vocabulary
2. Working out a trial translation
3. Correcting translations
4. Prayer drill
4. Story

You Know You've Succeeded When...

1. Students work out a reasonable translation of this text.
2. Students correct their translation.
3. Students discuss the connection of prayer and healing.

1. Introducing/Reviewing Vocabulary ■ [a] Using VOCABULARY POSTERS and FLASHCARDS, the teacher should introduce and drill the core vocabulary needed for this translation. [b] Some game playing or team competition is the perfect way to reinforce this vocabulary.

2. Working out a Trial Translation ■ [a] Working in pairs, students should develop their own best TRANSLATION of this text. [b] They should not worry about being perfect—they should worry about coming close. EXPECT a working translation something like:

Bless You Adonai, love nation Israel.

3. Correcting translations ■

• אוֹהֵב עַמּוֹ יִשְׂרָאֵל = "The Lover" of Israel

4. Prayer Drill ■ Practice performing this portion of the prayer. SING or READ it together.

5. Story ■

Review the vocabulary and make your best guess at the meaning of the חֲתִימָה of אַהֲבַת עוֹלָם

words

nation = עַם

word parts

and = ‍וֹ

יִשְׂרָאֵל
Israel

אֹהֵב
love

אַתָּה
You

בָּרֵךְ
bless

Take your best guess at the meaning of this text. Your teacher will help you with your translation.

בָּרוּךְ אַתָּה יי אוֹהֵב עַמּוֹ יִשְׂרָאֵל.

Bless You, Adonai, Who loves His People Israel

Rabbi Akiva and Rachel

Rabbi Akiva was a poor and ignorant shepherd working for a rich man, Kalba Savua. Akiva was forty years old and had not studied a word of Torah. He did not even know a Hebrew letter. Rachel, Kalba Savua's daughter, fell in love with Akiva. She said to him, "If I am willing to get engaged to you, will you go to a house of study?" Akiva answered, "Yes." So they were engaged in secret. When her father learned about it he drove her out of his house and cut her off. To get even she went and married Akiva. They were so poor that they had to sleep in straw. When

26

Rabbi Akiva picked the straw from her hair, he would say, "If I had the means, I would give you a golden hairpiece, 'a Jerusalem of gold.'"

The prophet Elijah came disguised as a beggar and asked, "Please give me a bit of straw—my wife is about to give birth, and I have nothing for her to lie on." Rabbi Akiva gave him some and said to his wife, "Look, this man doesn't even have the straw that we have!"

Soon Rachel told him, "Now is the time for you to go to learn Torah." He went and studied for twelve years. He had to start at the beginning. He went directly to a schoolhouse, and he and his son began reading from a child's tablet. Rabbi Akiva took hold of one end of the tablet, and his son held the other end. The teacher wrote down *alef* and *bet* for him, and he learned them; *alef* to *tav*, and he learned them; the book of Leviticus, and he learned it. He went on studying until he learned the whole Torah. At the end of twelve years he had become a leading scholar. He returned home bringing with him twelve thousand disciples. The whole town went out to meet him. Rachel went out to meet him, too. When she came near him, she fell upon her face and was about to kiss his feet. The disciples started to push her out of the way. Rabbi Akiva shouted at them, "Let her be—all I have and all that you have really belongs to her."

Her father fell upon his face before Rabbi Akiva. He gave Rabbi Akiva half of his wealth. Rabbi Akiva bought Rachel, his wife, a Jerusalem of Gold. *(Avot de Rabbi Natan 6, 12)*

Questions
1. What does this story teach us about the connection between "love" and "Torah?"
2. How does Rachel's love help Rabbi Akiva become a scholar?
3. How does God's love help us study Torah?
4. How does knowing the love story between Rabbi Akiva and Rachel help us to point our hearts when we say אַהֲבַת עוֹלָם?

27

STORY
The love story between Akiva and Rachel shows "a perfect love" with each taking care of the other's needs.

Big Ideas
1. Torah study is an important Jewish value.
2. Rachel sacrifices so that Akiva can study.
3. Akiva comes home and honors his wife.

Learning Activities
1. Read the story
2. Go over the story in Hevruta.
3. Discuss the questions

You Know You've Succeeded When...
1. Students can retell the story.
2. Student can provide reasonable answers to the questions.

1. **Read the Story** ■

2. **Go over the Story in Hevruta** ■

3. **Discuss the Questions** ■

1. **What does this story teach us about the connection between "love" and "Torah"?** That just as the Torah was given so it can be studied in love, and so can love lead to its study.

2. **How does Rachel's love help Rabbi Akiva become a scholar?** She sacrificed years of his company so that he could go and study.

3. **How does God's love help us study Torah?** Expect a variety of personal answers including "God makes us smart."

4. **How does knowing the love story about Rabbi Akiva and Rachel help us to point our hearts when we say אַהֲבַת עוֹלָם?** Expect personal answers such as "We can think of the Torah as a love story."

Blank Page

שְׁמַע

שְׁמַע is the "watchword of the Jewish faith." In this unit we will explore the text, meaning, language and process of the שְׁמַע.

Lesson 7

LESSON 7: שְׁמַע

This lesson looks at the שְׁמַע, the most important sentence in the prayerbook.

Big Ideas

1. The שְׁמַע is probably the most important sentence in the Torah because it states the single most important idea—that God is one.

2. The single sentence Deut. 6.4 (plus the בָּרוּךְ שֵׁם) is sometimes called the שְׁמַע. However, the (complete) שְׁמַע is made up of three paragraphs from different places in the Torah that were brought together to replace the Ten Commandments in the daily service.

3. The thing that the three paragraphs have in common is the phrase כָּל–מִצְוֹתַי, the idea of all the מִצְוֹת being important.

4. The שְׁמַע turns the love of God into actions. It teaches that people should live their belief in God by doing the things commanded in the Torah.

Learning Activities

1. Introducing the unit
2. Exploring the themes
3. Reviewing the key themes

You Know You've Succeeded When...

1. Students can describe the taking of the Torah out of the ark.
2. Students can state the two images that are used.

1. Introducing the Unit ■ Sing or say the שְׁמַע together. I'll bet most of your class can do it by heart. If you need a text to work from, it is on page 24 of the student text.

2. Exploring the Themes ■ CONVEY THE INFORMATION IN THE INTRODUCTION: Do one of the following. [a] DESCRIBE the information to your students. [b] READ out loud and DISCUSS this information. [c] ASSIGN your students to READ the information on their own and then DISCUSS it.

3. Reviewing the Key Themes ■

Question: How can you live the truth that God Is One? The simplest answer that the Torah is trying to teach is: by following the Torah and performing the מִצְוֹת.

We can also express this idea in other ways:

a. By treating all people as if they were created in the One God's image.

b. By being God's partner and working to make the world a better place for all people.

c. By living up to God's image and becoming the best person we can be.

d. By taking the love that God shows us and passing it on to other people.

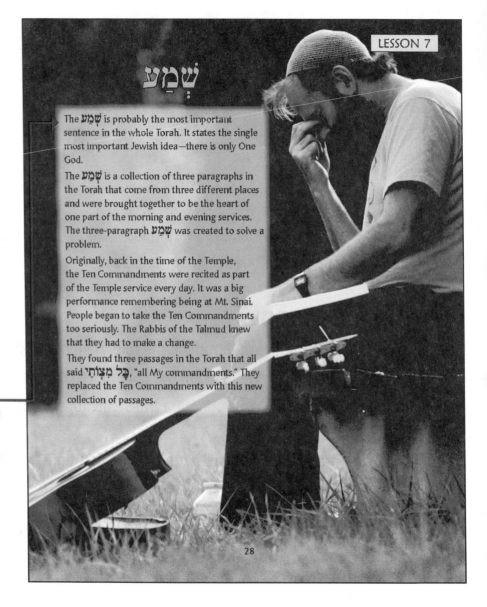

שְׁמַע

The שְׁמַע is probably the most important sentence in the whole Torah. It states the single most important Jewish idea—there is only One God.

The שְׁמַע is a collection of three paragraphs in the Torah that come from three different places and were brought together to be the heart of one part of the morning and evening services. The three-paragraph שְׁמַע was created to solve a problem.

Originally, back in the time of the Temple, the Ten Commandments were recited as part of the Temple service every day. It was a big performance remembering being at Mt. Sinai. People began to take the Ten Commandments too seriously. The Rabbis of the Talmud knew that they had to make a change.

They found three passages in the Torah that all said כָּל מִצְוֹתַי, "all My commandments." They replaced the Ten Commandments with this new collection of passages.

28

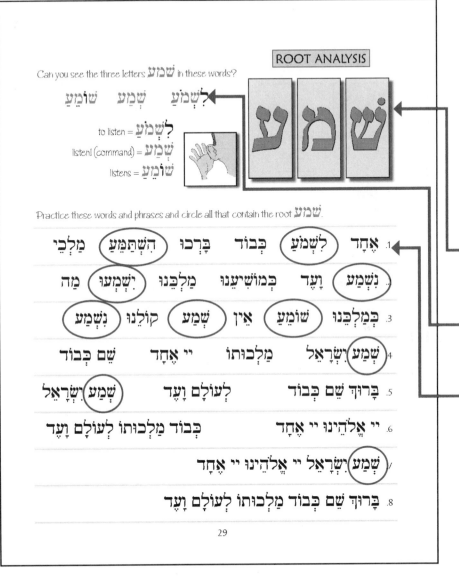

ROOT שָׁמַע

This page begins the study of roots by unpacking the root שָׁמַע.

Big Ideas

1. Mastering Hebrew roots dramatically improves comprehension.
2. Looking at words built out of a single root enhances an understanding of Hebrew thinking.

Learning Activities

1. Analysis of the root שָׁמַע
2. Identifying words built out of שָׁמַע
3. Reading and identifying activity

You Know You've Succeeded When...

• Students can identify words with a שָׁמַע root.

1. Analysis of the Root שָׁמַע ■

a. Use the board or flashcards to introduce the root שָׁמַע and the words built out of it.

b. Establish the connection between the three words: לִשְׁמֹע, שְׁמַע, שׁוֹמֵעַ. NOTE: "Listen" is the core idea.

2. Identifying Words Built out of שָׁמַע ■

a. ASK: What word idea connects שׁוֹמֵעַ, שְׁמַע, לִשְׁמֹע?

b. ESTABLISH that these are the same words with differing tenses.

3. Reading and Identifying Activity ■

a. Let students prepare these lines with a Hevruta partner.

b. Go over the passage. Invite individual students to read. Ask the entire class to read out together the words built out of the root שָׁמַע.

TEXT, TRANSLATION & COMMENTARY

This page continues the Hebrew and English text of שְׁמַע. It should be used for both introducing the prayer and perfecting its performance.

Big Ideas

1. Growing and reinforcing Hebrew vocabulary leads to a growing affinity with the liturgy.
2. Applying the Hebrew they have to form rough translations of Hebrew prayers (a) helps students to feel closer to those texts, (b) reinforces the Hebrew they are learning and (c) develops a process they can continue to apply to the Siddur.
3. Choreography of the שְׁמַע.

Learning Activities

1. Introducing/reviewing vocabulary
2. Working out a trial translation
3. Correcting translations
4. Prayer drill
5. Discussing commentary

You Know You've Succeeded When...

1. Students work out a reasonable translation of this text.
2. Students correct their translation.
3. Students unpack the choreography of the שְׁמַע.

1. Introducing/Reviewing Vocabulary ■ [a] Using VOCABULARY POSTERS and FLASHCARDS, introduce and drill the core vocabulary needed for this translation. [b] Some game playing or team competition is the perfect way to reinforce this vocabulary.

2. Working out a Trial Translation ■ [a] Working in pairs, students should develop their own best TRANSLATION. [b] They should not worry about being perfect—they should worry about coming close. EXPECT a working translation something like:

Listen Israel, Adonai our God, One Adonai
Bless name heavy—his king—world and more.

3. Correcting Translations ■

- מַלְכוּת means "kingdom" rather than "king"
- עוֹלָם means "eternity" rather than "world"
- נוּ Ending: You may want to review the fact that אֱלֹהֵינוּ = נוּ + אֱלֹהִים.
- On the vocabulary side we have the word כָּבֵד (heavy), but the word in the prayer is כָּבוֹד (honor). Point out that they come from the same root. Ask about the connection. The answer: Something we honor is something we treat as "heavy" (with weight).

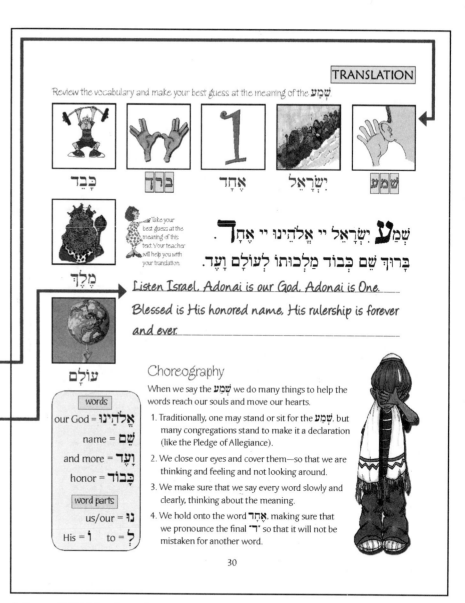

TRANSLATION

Review the vocabulary and make your best guess at the meaning of the שְׁמַע.

כָּבֵד   בָּרוּךְ   אֶחָד   יִשְׂרָאֵל   שְׁמַע

מֶלֶךְ

עוֹלָם

Take your best guess at the meaning of this text. Your teacher will help you with your translation.

שְׁמַע יִשְׂרָאֵל יי אֱלֹהֵינוּ יי אֶחָד.
בָּרוּךְ שֵׁם כְּבוֹד מַלְכוּתוֹ לְעוֹלָם וָעֶד.

<u>Listen Israel, Adonai is our God, Adonai is One.</u>
<u>Blessed is His honored name, His rulership is forever</u>
<u>and ever.</u>

words	
our God =	אֱלֹהֵינוּ
name =	שֵׁם
and more =	וָעֶד
honor =	כְּבוֹד

word parts	
us/our =	נוּ
His =	וֹ to =	לְ

Choreography

When we say the שְׁמַע we do many things to help the words reach our souls and move our hearts.

1. Traditionally, one may stand or sit for the שְׁמַע, but many congregations stand to make it a declaration (like the Pledge of Allegiance).
2. We close our eyes and cover them—so that we are thinking and feeling and not looking around.
3. We make sure that we say every word slowly and clearly, thinking about the meaning.
4. We hold onto the word אֶחָד, making sure that we pronounce the final "ד" so that it will not be mistaken for another word.

30

4. Prayer Drill ■ Practice performing this portion of the prayer. SING or READ it together.

5. Discussing Commentary ■ READ and DISCUSS the choreography.

Read these directions as a class. Stand up and practice the שְׁמַע.

The שְׁמַע Rebuilds the Temple

Sometimes a whole story can be told in a sentence. The Temple was the place where the Jewish people came close to God. Three times a year every Jew would come up to Jerusalem, up to the Temple. The Temple was a very big place, but it was not actually big enough to fit all of the Jewish people. We are told that on those days the Temple would stretch to make sure that there was room for everyone.

Here is the one-sentence story. Everywhere else in the world Jews answered a prayer with "אָמֵן," but in the Temple, people answered, "בָּרוּךְ שֵׁם כְּבוֹד מַלְכוּתוֹ לְעוֹלָם וָעֶד."

אָמֵן means "me, too." It is a way of saying, "I believe what he or she said." When you say "אָמֵן" God gives you credit for saying the prayer you've heard another person say. When the Rabbis added the בָּרוּךְ שֵׁם to the שְׁמַע, they made that one prayer a time when every Jew was again in the Temple. When we say בָּרוּךְ שֵׁם, we know that we are One People—connected to the One God.

Questions
1. What was the original purpose of the בָּרוּךְ שֵׁם?
2. How did it change the שְׁמַע?
3. What is "Oneness" in this story?
4. How can knowing this one-sentence story help you point your heart when you say the שְׁמַע?

31

STORY: THE שְׁמַע REBUILDS THE TEMPLE

This is the third explanation of why the בָּרוּךְ שֵׁם was added to the שְׁמַע. This explanation from the Talmud states that the בָּרוּךְ שֵׁם was a prayer said only in the Temple—it was added to שְׁמַע after the Temple was destroyed to remind us that there was (and will again be) a place where all Jews could come together.

Big Ideas
- אֶחָד in the שְׁמַע reminds us that כָּל יִשְׂרָאֵל עֲרֵבִין זֶה בָּזֶה *kol yisrael avrevim zeh ba-zeh*—all Israel is interconnected—We are One!

Learning Activities
1. Read the Story
2. Go over the story in Hevruta.
3. Discuss the Questions

You Know You've Succeeded When...
1. Students can retell the story.
2. Student can provide reasonable answers to the questions.

1. Read the story ■

2. Go over the story in Hevruta ■

3. Discuss the questions ■

1. **What was the original purpose of the בָּרוּךְ שֵׁם?** It was a special version of "amen" used in the Temple.

2. **How did it change the שְׁמַע?** It gave the שְׁמַע a Temple connection. Now every time we say the שְׁמַע we remember a time when we were a huge Jewish community and we hope for the time when this can happen again.

3. **What is the "Oneness" in this story?** There may be many different answers to this question. Allow for a lot of interesting interpretations, but the core idea is that it reminds us that the Jewish people are one.

4. **How can knowing this one-sentence story help you point your heart when you say the שְׁמַע?** Again, there can be lots of wonderful responses, because כַּוָּנָה is a personal thing. The core idea here is that a vision of the unity of the Jewish people can help us to talk about the unity of God.

STORY

This third "true" story expands the story on the other page. This one is built on the image of rebuilding the Temple. The part of the story that may be hard for students (especially in Reform and Conservative congregations) is that the idea of rebuilding the Temple may not be that positive an image. You will need to explain that one of the prayers in the daily service is the request that God send the Messiah and rebuild the Temple. You will need to explain that the rebuilding of the Temple is a hope that all of the exile and hurt in the world will come to an end, and things will finally be better.

Big Ideas

• By saying the בָּרוּךְ שֵׁם and by remembering a time when Israel was One, we are beginning the process of making Israel one again

Learning Activities

1. Read the Story
2. Go over the story in Hevruta.
3. Discuss the Questions

You Know You've Succeeded When...

1. Students can retell the story.
2. Student can provide reasonable answers to the questions.

1. Read the story ■

2. Go over the story in Hevruta ■

3. Discuss the questions ■

1. **How was the Temple made whole?** The boy in the story imagined it.

2. **How is the בָּרוּךְ שֵׁם in the שְׁמַע the same as the closed eyes in this story?** We are remembering a time when the Temple was one, and we are wishing for a time when we can again come together as one people—completely.

   The modern State of Israel is part of this connection, but the world still has a lot of "exile" in it. It is not yet redeemed.

Latifa Kropf told this story. A boy comes to his teacher, Mimi Feigelson, and starts to cry. She asks him what is wrong, and he explains that he has been praying and praying for the Temple to be rebuilt. He is upset that his prayers did not work, the Temple remains broken.

He says, "God doesn't answer me."

The teacher asks the boy to close his eyes. She says, "Imagine that the Temple has become whole."

The boy closes his eyes, and slowly a great smile fills his face. Finally he opens his eyes and says, "Teacher, I saw it—I really saw it—the Temple whole."

The teacher smiles at him and says, "Your prayers were answered."

Questions

1. How was the Temple made whole?
2. How is the בָּרוּךְ שֵׁם in the שְׁמַע the same as the closed eyes in this story?

32

32

וְאָהַבְתָּ

וְאָהַבְתָּ is the rest of the first paragraph of the שְׁמַע. In this unit we will explore the text, meaning, language and process of the וְאָהַבְתָּ.

Lesson 8

Page 27: We introduce the role, theme and imagery of the וְאָהַבְתָּ.

Page 28: We look at a text and translation of the וְאָהַבְתָּ.

Page 29: The second page of the text and translation.

Page 30: We translate the first sentence of the וְאָהַבְתָּ part of the שְׁמַע. Because of the word כָּל in this sentence, we look at the קָמַץ קָטָן.

Lesson 9

Page 31: We translate the last part of the וְאָהַבְתָּ.

Page 32: We connect the final two sentences of וְאָהַבְתָּ to the mezuzah.

Page 33: We read the story of the death of Rabbi Akiva.

Blank Page

וְאָהַבְתָּ

The וְאָהַבְתָּ is:

- part of the first paragraph of the שְׁמַע, or
- the prayer that comes after the שְׁמַע.

The וְאָהַבְתָּ continues the idea that God is our God. It teaches us that

- we should love God,
- the way to show our love is by studying and living Torah,
- מִצְוֹת are the way we live Torah,
- there are מִצְוֹת we can do at all times of the day (every day),
- there are מִצְוֹת we can do anywhere and everywhere we go,
- some Jewish things we do help us to remember the מִצְוֹת,
- teaching Torah to our children is a very important מִצְוָה.

Some congregations say three paragraphs of the שְׁמַע in their service, some say only one.

Those that say only one take the last line of the third paragraph and put it on the ending of the וְאָהַבְתָּ. This is the part that tells us that by doing the מִצְוֹת we become קָדוֹשׁ, holy.

LESSON 8: וְאָהַבְתָּ

This lesson looks at the וְאָהַבְתָּ.

Big Ideas

1. There are two different ways of labeling this prayer. It can be the first paragraph of the שְׁמַע or it can be the וְאָהַבְתָּ.
2. We express our love of God through performing מִצְוֹת.

Learning Activities

1. Introducing the unit
2. Exploring the themes
3. Reviewing the key themes

You Know You've Succeeded When...

1. Students can describe how the וְאָהַבְתָּ is labeled and performed in your synagogue.
2. Students can describe the major lessons of the וְאָהַבְתָּ.

1. Introducing the Unit.

2. Exploring the Themes ■ CONVEY THE INFORMATION IN THE INTRODUCTION: Do one of the following. [a] DESCRIBE the information to your students. [b] READ out loud and DISCUSS this information or [c] ASSIGN your students to READ the information on their own and then DISCUSS it.

3. Reviewing the Key Themes ■

These are the core concepts in this overview.

- How can one fulfill the commandment to love God? The simplest answer the Torah is trying to teach is that by following the Torah and performing the commandments (מִצְוֹת) we can love God.

But we can also express this idea in other ways:

- By treating all people as if they were created in the One God's image.
- By being God's partner and working to make the world a better place for all people.
- By living up to God's image and becoming the best person we can be.
- By taking the love that God shows us and passing it on to other people.

Your students may find may other interesting ways of expressing this idea.

TEXT, TRANSLATION & COMMENTARY

This page contains the Hebrew and English text of וְאָהַבְתָּ. It should be used for both introducing the prayer and perfecting its performance.

Big Ideas

1. When we enable students to perfect performances of core liturgy we make it possible for them to far more easily participate in communal worship.
2. By scanning the English of prayers students can grow insights into the meaning of the liturgy.

Learning Activities

1. Scanning the English text
2. Practicing the Hebrew text

You Know You've Succeeded When...

1. Students describe insights gained from looking at the English text.
2. Students practice their performance of the Hebrew text.
3. Students read, discuss and respond to the commentary.

1. Scanning the English Text ■ INVITE students to SCAN the English translation of these prayers. ASK them what "big ideas" they can find by looking. INSIGHTS that might be shared:

- We have an obligation to love God. (How do we do this? The traditional answer—through doing the מִצְוֹת.)
- The Torah (מִצְוֹת) is supposed to be part of everything we do.
- The מִצְוֹת can make us holy.

2. Practicing the Hebrew Text ■ [a] INVITE students to work with a partner and practice the prayer. [b] READ or SING the prayers together as a class. [c] INVITE individual students or teams of students to perform individual lines or sections.

Notes: These notes are for the teacher; they should be used to enrich one of the repetitions of this page.

Maimonides taught that you can find three things in the first paragraph of the שְׁמַע: (1) a statement of belief (line 2); (2) a commitment to love God (lines 5-8); (3) a commitment to live a life of Torah (lines 13-21).

The Torah speaks of Heart-Love, Soul-Love and Stuff-Love. We are inviting students to create their own categories here. The traditional understanding, however, is that Heart-Love equals "feelings," Soul-Love is "what you are willing to die for" and Stuff-Love is "on what you are willing to spend money." This understanding can be found in Rashi on this passage in chapter 6 of Deuteronomy.

וְאָהַבְתָּ

LISTEN, ISRAEL,	1. שְׁמַע יִשְׂרָאֵל
ADONAI is our God, ADONAI is the ONE (and only) God.	2. יי אֱלֹהֵינוּ יי אֶחָד.
BLESSED be the NAME—that God's HONORED EMPIRE	3. בָּרוּךְ שֵׁם כְּבוֹד מַלְכוּתוֹ
will last FOREVER and ALWAYS.	4. לְעוֹלָם וָעֶד.
You should LOVE ADONAI your God	5. וְאָהַבְתָּ אֵת יי אֱלֹהֶיךָ
with all your HEART	6. בְּכָל לְבָבְךָ
with all your SOUL	7. וּבְכָל נַפְשְׁךָ
with all your STUFF.	8. וּבְכָל מְאֹדֶךָ.
And these THINGS that	9. וְהָיוּ הַדְּבָרִים הָאֵלֶּה
I make MITZVOT for you today	10. אֲשֶׁר אָנֹכִי מְצַוְּךָ הַיּוֹם
shall be on your HEART.	11. עַל לְבָבֶךָ.
You should TEACH them to your children	12. וְשִׁנַּנְתָּם לְבָנֶיךָ
and you should TALK about them	13. וְדִבַּרְתָּ בָּם
when you SIT at home	14. בְּשִׁבְתְּךָ בְּבֵיתֶךָ
when you are GOING out	15. וּבְלֶכְתְּךָ בַדֶּרֶךְ
when you LIE down	16. וּבְשָׁכְבְּךָ
and when you get UP.	17. וּבְקוּמֶךָ
And you should TIE them as LETTERS on your HAND	18. וּקְשַׁרְתָּם לְאוֹת עַל יָדֶךָ
And have them as SYMBOLS between your EYES.	19. וְהָיוּ לְטֹטָפוֹת בֵּין עֵינֶיךָ.

34

Hebrew Text

Know that these lines, from לְמַעַן תִּזְכְּרוּ on, come from the third paragraph of the שְׁמַע. The Reform movement makes them part of their one-paragraph compilation.

And you should WRITE them on the DOORPOSTS of your HOUSE	וּכְתַבְתָּם עַל־מְזֻזוֹת בֵּיתֶךָ	20.
and on your GATES.	וּבִשְׁעָרֶיךָ.	21.
That you will REMEMBER	לְמַעַן תִּזְכְּרוּ	22.
and DO all My MITZVOT	וַעֲשִׂיתֶם אֶת־כָּל־מִצְוֹתָי	23.
and BE HOLY for your God.	וִהְיִיתֶם קְדֹשִׁים לֵאלֹהֵיכֶם.	24.
I am ADONAI, your God,	אֲנִי יי אֱלֹהֵיכֶם	25.
The One-Who-BROUGHT-you-OUT	אֲשֶׁר הוֹצֵאתִי אֶתְכֶם	26.
from the Land of Egypt	מֵאֶרֶץ מִצְרַיִם	27.
to BE your God	לִהְיוֹת לָכֶם לֵאלֹהִים	28.
I am ADONAI your God. FOR SURE.	אֲנִי יי אֱלֹהֵיכֶם. אֱמֶת.	29.

35

TRANSLATION

This page has students work on a translation of the first sentence of the וְאָהַבְתָּ.

Big Ideas

1. Growing and reinforcing Hebrew vocabulary leads to a growing affinity with the liturgy.
2. Applying the Hebrew they have to form rough translations of Hebrew prayers (a) helps students to feel closer to those texts, (b) reinforces the Hebrew they are learning and (c) develops a process they can continue to apply to the Siddur.
3. The קָמֵץ קָטָן

Learning Activities

1. Introducing/reviewing vocabulary
2. Working out a trial translation
3. Correcting translations
4. Prayer drill
5. The קָמֵץ קָטָן

You Know You've Succeeded When...

1. Students work out a reasonable translation of this text.
2. Students correct their translation.
3. Students can successfully read words with a קָמֵץ קָטָן.

1. Introducing/Reviewing Vocabulary ■ [a] Using VOCABULARY POSTERS and FLASHCARDS, introduce and drill the core vocabulary needed for this translation. [b] Some game playing or team competition is the perfect way to reinforce this vocabulary.

2. Working out a Trial Translation ■ [a] Working in pairs, students should develop their own best TRANSLATION. [b] They should not worry about being perfect—they should worry about coming close. EXPECT a working translation something like:

And you love Adonai Your God
With all your heart, with all your soul
and with all your might.

3. Correcting Translations ■

- מְאֹד means "stuff."
- ךָ Ending: You may want to review the fact that נַפְשְׁךָ = ךָ + נֶפֶשׁ.

4. Prayer Drill ■ Practice performing this portion of the prayer. SING or READ it together.

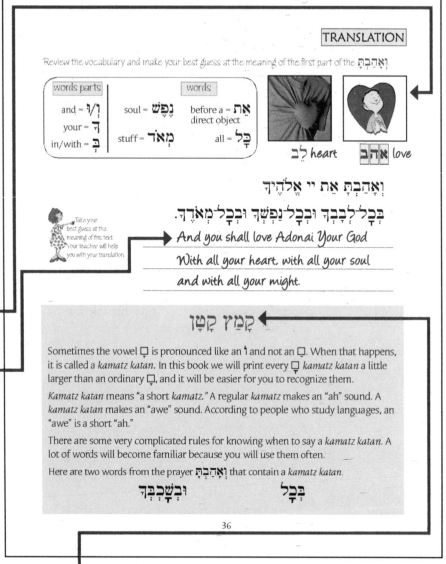

5. קָמֵץ קָטָן ■ READ about and DISCUSS the קָמֵץ קָטָן.
Point out to your students that in this book and in some Siddurim, every קָמֵץ קָטָן is made a little bit bigger or different to make it easier to see.

LESSON 9

TRANSLATION

Review the vocabulary and make your best guess at the meaning of the end of the וְאָהַבְתָּ

write כָּתַב	eyes עֵינַיִם	hand/arm יָד	signs אוֹתִיּוֹת	tie/bind קָשַׁר

mezuzah מְזוּזָה

Take your best guess at the meaning of this text. Your teacher will help you with your translation.

וּקְשַׁרְתָּם לְאוֹת עַל־יָדֶךָ

וְהָיוּ לְטֹטָפֹת בֵּין עֵינֶיךָ.

וּכְתַבְתָּם עַל־מְזֻזוֹת בֵּיתֶךָ וּבִשְׁעָרֶיךָ.

house בַּיִת

And tie into letters on your hands

And they shall be symbols between your eyes

And write them on the mezuzah your house and your gate

gate שַׁעַר

word parts		words	
your = ךָ	and = וְ/וּ	symbols = טֹטָפֹת	on = עַל
in/with = בְּ	to = לְ	between = בֵּין	they shall be = הָיוּ

37

LESSON 9: TRANSLATION

This page has students work on a translation of the final sentences of the וְאָהַבְתָּ.

Big Ideas

1. Growing and reinforcing Hebrew vocabulary leads to a growing affinity with the liturgy.
2. Applying the Hebrew they have to form rough translations of Hebrew prayers (a) helps students to feel closer to those texts, (b) reinforces the Hebrew they are learning and (c) develops a process they can continue to apply to the Siddur.

Learning Activities

1. Introducing/reviewing vocabulary
2. Working out a trial translation
3. Correcting translations
4. Prayer drill

You Know You've Succeeded When...

1. Students work out a reasonable translation of this text.
2. Students correct their translation.

1. Introducing/Reviewing Vocabulary ■ [a] Using VOCABULARY POSTERS and FLASHCARDS, introduce and drill the core vocabulary needed for this translation. [b] Some game playing or team competition is the perfect way to reinforce this vocabulary.

2. Working out a Trial Translation ■ [a] Working in pairs, students should develop their own best TRANSLATION. [b] They should not worry about being perfect—they should worry about coming close. EXPECT a working translation something like:

And tie into letters on your hands
And they shall be symbols between your eyes
And write them on the mezuzah your house and your gate

3. Correcting Translations ■

1. מְזוּזָה is not just the thing you put on the doorpost, but the doorpost itself.
2. שְׁעָרֶיךָ is plural—your gates

4. Prayer Drill ■ Practice performing this portion of the prayer. SING or READ it together.

MEZUZAH

Big Ideas

1. The mezuzah is the fulfillment of a biblical commandment.
2. The mezuzah teaches people about God.
3. It is a tradition to kiss the mezuzah and bring its words to our lips.

Learning Activities

1. Read the text
2. Discuss the big ideas

You Know You've Succeeded When...

1. Students can summarize the key points of the text.
2. Student can provide reasonable answers to the questions included in this guide.

1. Read the Story ■

2. Discuss These Questions ■

1. **What rules regulate the mezuzah?**
   a. Text is handwritten in 22 lines.
   b. Slanted position near top of door with top slanted inward
   c. On top of the outside of the parchment is written שַׁדַּי.

2. **What does Josephus say about the mezuzah?** It shows the greatest things God does for us.

3. **What does Maimonides teach about the mezuzah?** It shows that God is one and that God is everywhere.

4. **What is the meaning the custom of kissing the mezuzah?** It is designed to show that we are bringing the words of the mezuzah to our lips—taking them in.

Mezuzah

In the book of Deuteronomy we are told, "And you shall write them on the doorposts of your house and on your gates." The verse became the root of the practice of hanging a mezuzah on the doorway of every Jewish home. The mezuzah is a handwritten on parchment copy of the שְׁמַע that has twenty-two lines. The text is then placed in a box or tube. The mezuzah is placed in a slanting position, to the upper part of the right-hand door-post, so that the upper part is inward and the lower part outward. On the top of the outside of the parchment is written God's name, שַׁדַּי.

The Jewish historian Josephus explains the mezuzah by saying, "The greatest things God does for us are to be written on the doors... in order to show everywhere the good and the kindness that God does for us." Maimonides, the Jewish philosopher, adds: "From the mezuzah people learn when coming or going, that God is one and everywhere."

It is a tradition to touch the mezuzah and then touch our lips, bringing its words to our lips. When we hang a mezuzah we say this blessing:

בָּרוּךְ אַתָּה יי אֱלֹהֵינוּ מֶלֶךְ הָעוֹלָם אֲשֶׁר קִדְּשָׁנוּ
בְּמִצְוֹתָיו וְצִוָּנוּ לִקְבֹּעַ מְזוּזָה.

Death of Rabbi Akiva

The Roman government wanted to get even with the Jews for the rebellion led by Bar Kokhba. They made a rule forbidding the Jews from studying and practicing the Torah. Papas ben Judah came found Rabbi Akiva holding public Torah lessons; Papas asked Akiva, "Aren't you afraid of the government?" Rabbi Akiva replied: "Listen to this parable: A fox was walking on a river bank near some fish. He asked them, 'Why are you fleeing?' They replied, 'From the nets that people set.' So the fox said to them, 'How about coming up on dry land, so that we can live together?' They replied, 'No way. If we are afraid to be in a place where we can stay alive, we should be more afraid to be in a place where we are sure to die!' So it is with us. If we are afraid to sit and study the Torah how much more afraid should we be to stop studying Torah!"

Rabbi Akiva was arrested and thrown into prison. When Rabbi Akiva was taken out to be executed it was time to say the שְׁמַע. The executioners were combing his flesh with iron combs, yet there was a smile on his face. His students asked: "Why is this happening?" He said: "All my life I have been troubled by this Torah verse 'With all thy soul' (Deut. 6:5), which I have interpreted as meaning 'Even if God takes your soul.' But I said: 'When shall I have a chance to fulfill that mitzvah?' Now I have a chance to do it." He stretched out the last word of the שְׁמַע—אֶחָד ("one")—until he died as he finished saying it. It was his last breath. (Brakhot 61b)

Questions

1. How does Torah keep Jews alive?
2. What did Rabbi Akiva learn about the שְׁמַע when he died?
3. What do you think "loving God with all your heart" and "loving God with all your stuff" involves?
4. How can knowing this story help you to point your heart when you say the וְאָהַבְתָּ?

39

DEATH OF RABBI AKIVA

Akiva teaches that Jews cannot survive without the Torah and then is killed for practicing that truth. He died living the teaching of the וְאָהַבְתָּ that we should love Torah בְּכָל נַפְשְׁךָ with all our soul.

Big Ideas

1. Jews cannot survive without Torah.
2. Jews need to be ready to die for Torah.

Learning Activities

1. Read the story
2. Go over the story in Hevruta.
3. Discuss the questions

You Know You've Succeeded When...

1. Students can retell the story.
2. Students can provide reasonable answers to the questions.

1. Read the Story ■

2. Go over the Story in Hevruta ■

3. Discuss the Questions ■

1. **How does Torah keep Jews alive?** Torah keep the "Jewish part" of Jews alive. Torah is about spiritual life.

2. **What did Rabbi Akiva learn about the שְׁמַע when he died?** He learned that he had the strength to "love God with all his soul."

3. **What do you think "loving God with all your heart" and "loving God with all your stuff" involves?** This question invites traditional interpretations. The Gemora explains that "loving God with all your heart" means loving God with all of your feeling—devoting all of your feelings to God's service. And the Gemora explains that "loving God with all of your stuff" involves using your wealth for God's agenda.

4. **How can knowing this story help you to point your heart when you say the וְאָהַבְתָּ?** This calls for a personal answer.

Blank Page

מִי כָמֹכָה

This two-lesson unit finishes the cycle of the שְׁמַע and her blessings. We will look at the thematic, structural and linguistic patterns in this prayer and work on practicing its performance.

Lesson 10

Lesson 11

LESSON 10: מִי כָמֹכָה

These are the core concepts in this overview.

Big Idea

1. מִי כָמֹכָה comes from the Torah. It is a poem sung by the Israelites at the crossing of the Reed Sea.
2. This song is placed in the middle of a prayer called the גְּאֻלָּה (The Redemption)—the blessing that comes after the שְׁמַע in the morning service.
3. The theme of the גְּאֻלָּה is that the Exodus from Egypt is both a memory of one time that God redeemed (saved) us and a proof that God will redeem us in the future.

Learning Activities

1. Introducing the unit
2. Exploring the themes
3. Reviewing the key themes

You Know You've Succeeded When...

1. Students can describe the the scene of the Israelites at the Reed Sea as part of the Exodus from Egypt.
2. Sudents can state the images that are used.

1. Introducing the Unit ■ READ the introduction.

2. Exploring the Themes ■ CONVEY THE INFORMATION IN THE INTRODUCTION: Do one of the following. [a] DESCRIBE the information to your students. [b] READ out loud and DISCUSS this information or [c] ASSIGN your students to READ the information on their own and then DISCUSS it.

3. Reviewing the Key Themes ■

These are the core concepts:

1. מִי כָמֹכָה comes from the Torah. It is a poem sung by the Israelites at the crossing of the Reed Sea.

2. This song is placed in the middle of a prayer called the גְּאֻלָּה (The Redemption)—the blessing that comes after the שְׁמַע in the morning service.

   Redemption: One of the tasks you will need to do here is to define "redemption." Literally, to "redeem" something is to "restore" it. When we were slaves in Egypt, God "redeemed" us and brought us to freedom. In general usage, redeem means to save or to rescue. The final redemption is when God (with our help) perfects and heals the world.

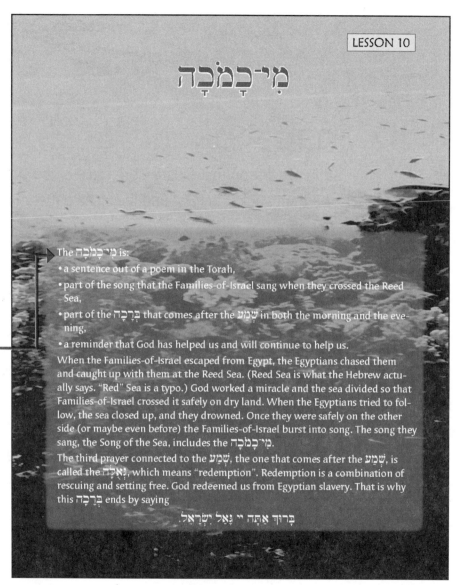

LESSON 10

מִי־כָמֹכָה

The מִי־כָמֹכָה is:
- a sentence out of a poem in the Torah,
- part of the song that the Families-of-Israel sang when they crossed the Reed Sea,
- part of the בְּרָכָה that comes after the שְׁמַע in both the morning and the evening,
- a reminder that God has helped us and will continue to help us.

When the Families-of-Israel escaped from Egypt, the Egyptians chased them and caught up with them at the Reed Sea. (Reed Sea is what the Hebrew actually says. "Red" Sea is a typo.) God worked a miracle and the sea divided so that Families-of-Israel crossed it safely on dry land. When the Egyptians tried to follow, the sea closed up, and they drowned. Once they were safely on the other side (or maybe even before) the Families-of-Israel burst into song. The song they sang, the Song of the Sea, includes the מִי־כָמֹכָה.

The third prayer connected to the שְׁמַע, the one that comes after the שְׁמַע, is called the גְּאֻלָּה, which means "redemption". Redemption is a combination of rescuing and setting free. God redeemed us from Egyptian slavery. That is why this בְּרָכָה ends by saying

בָּרוּךְ אַתָּה יי גָּאַל יִשְׂרָאֵל.

3. The theme of the גְּאֻלָּה is that the Exodus from Egypt is both a memory of one time that God redeemed (saved) us and a proof that God will redeem us in the future.

גְּאֻלָה

Moses and the Families-of-Israel	1. מֹשֶׁה וּבְנֵי יִשְׂרָאֵל
responded to You in very happy song	2. לְךָ עָנוּ שִׁירָה בְּשִׂמְחָה רַבָּה,
and they all said:	3. וְאָמְרוּ כֻלָּם:
Which of the other (false) gods is like You, ADONAI	4. מִי־כָמֹכָה בָּאֵלִם יי,
Who is like You, GLORIOUS in holiness	5. מִי כָּמֹכָה נֶאְדָּר בַּקֹּדֶשׁ,
AWESOME in praises, DOING miracles?	6. נוֹרָא תְהִלֹּת עֹשֵׂה פֶלֶא.
Your FAMILIES saw Your RULE	7. מַלְכוּתְךָ רָאוּ בָנֶיךָ
when You DIVIDED the sea before MOSES:	8. בּוֹקֵעַ יָם לִפְנֵי מֹשֶׁה
"This is MY GOD" they answered and said	9. זֶה אֵלִי עָנוּ וְאָמְרוּ
ADONAI will rule forever and ever.	10. יי יִמְלֹךְ לְעֹלָם וָעֶד.
And it is written:	11. וְנֶאֱמַר:
"ADONAI will FREE JACOB	12. כִּי פָדָה יי אֶת־יַעֲקֹב,
and REDEEM him from a hand	13. וּגְאָלוֹ מִיַּד
mightier than his own."	14. חָזָק מִמֶּנּוּ.
BLESSED be You, ADONAI	15. בָּרוּךְ אַתָּה יי
The ONE Who REDEEMED Israel.	16. גָּאַל יִשְׂרָאֵל.

TEXT, TRANSLATION & COMMENTARY

This text is only a portion of the full גְּאֻלָה. These are the portions that are sung at the end of the longer passage. These are the portions that are sung together. You should think about moving from reading into singing, if that is within your skill range.

Big Ideas

1. When we enable students to perfect performances of core liturgy we make it possible for them to far more easily participate in communal worship.

2. By scanning the English of prayers students can grow insights into the meaning of the liturgy.

Learning Activities

1. Scanning the English text
2. Practicing the Hebrew text

You Know You've Succeeded When...

1. Students describe insights gained from looking at the English text.
2. Students practice their performance of the Hebrew text.
3. Students read, discuss and respond to the commentary.

1. Scanning the English Text ■ INVITE students to SCAN the English translation of these prayers. ASK them what "big ideas" they can find by looking. INSIGHTS that might be shared:

- God will redeem us, save us and make things better.
- The Exodus is our proof that God is real. It shows a time in history when God directly came into our lives. But it is also a projection of a time when we—using Torah as our guide—can make the oneness of God real for all people through the creation of a final redemption.
- The מִי כָמֹכָה is a recreation—an acting out of the song sung by Moses and Miriam and the people on the banks of the Reed Sea. By reliving it, we begin to make it part of our future.

2. Practicing the Hebrew Text ■ [a] INVITE students to work with a partner and practice the prayer. [b] READ or SING the prayers together as a class. [c] INVITE individual students or teams of students to perform individual lines or sections.

TRANSLATION/COMMENTARY

This page has students work on a translation of מִי כָמֹכָה.

Big Ideas

1. Growing and reinforcing Hebrew vocabulary leads to a growing affinity with the liturgy.
2. Applying the Hebrew they have to form rough translations of Hebrew prayers (a) helps students to feel closer to those texts, (b) reinforces the Hebrew they are learning and (c) develops a process they can continue to apply to the Siddur.

Learning Activities

1. Working out a trial translation
2. Correcting translations
3. Prayer drill

You Know You've Succeeded When...

1 Students work out a reasonable translation of this text.
2. Students correct their translation.

1. Working out a Trial Translation ■ [a] Working in pairs, students should develop their own best TRANSLATION. [b] They should not worry about being perfect—they should worry about coming close. EXPECT a working translation something like:

Who is like (You) in the gods Adonai
Who is like (You) splendor in holiness
Awesome praises make wonder.

2. Correcting Translations ■

- כָמֹכָה will not read as "Like you." It will be good to tell them that ךָ = כָה.
- נֶאְדָּר בַּקֹדֶשׁ—splendorous or glorious in holinesss. This will take just a little sanding.
- Likewise, נוֹרָא תְהִלֹת עֹשֵׂה פֶלֶא will take a few words here and there to come out as English.

3. Prayer Drill ■ Practice performing this portion of the prayer. SING or READ it together.

Your teacher will help you with your translation.

מִי־כָמֹכָה בָּאֵלִם יי
מִי כָּמֹכָה נֶאְדָּר בַּקֹדֶשׁ
נוֹרָא תְהִלֹת עֹשֵׂה פֶלֶא

Who is like (You) in the gods Adonai

Who is like (You) splendor in holiness

Awesome praises make wonder.

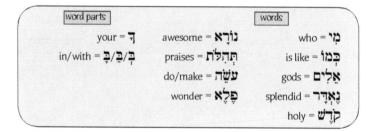

word parts		words
your = ךָ	awesome = נוֹרָא	who = מִי
in/with = בְּ/בַּ/בָּ	praises = תְהִלֹת	is like = כְּמוֹ
	do/make = עֹשֵׂה	gods = אֵלִם
	wonder = פֶלֶא	splendid = נֶאְדָּר
		holy = קֹדֶשׁ

42

LESSON 11

The Women Hold Hands

Here is another story of how the Reed Sea divided. Every tribe wanted to be the first to enter the water. Each tribe wanted the bragging rights, so they prevented every other tribe from getting wet. It looked like a huge rugby game with everyone pushing and holding each other back. While the men were busy struggling, the women looked at each other. They nodded and stepped back a little. They took each other's hands and worked their way around the men. They counted together, and on the count of three the women-of-Israel stepped into the sea all at once. The second they entered, the sea divided. When that happened, the men stopped struggling with each other and all of Israel began to cross. (From the Midrash)

Questions
1. What did the women figure out about what God wants from us?
2. What is the lesson of this midrash?
3. How can remembering the story of the women help us to point our hearts when we say the מִי־כָמֹכָה?

43

LESSON 11: A STORY "THE WOMEN HOLD HANDS"

In this story, the men fight for the honor of being the first to enter the sea while the women realize that cooperation is the way to make miracles. This is the opposite of the Nahshon story. Rather than needing a leader, sometimes miracles take the participation of everyone.

 Big Ideas
1. Cooperation is a way to work miracles.
2. We worked together to get out of Egypt.

 Learning Activities
1. Read the story
2. Go over the story in Hevruta.
3. Discuss the questions

 You Know You've Succeeded When...
1. Students can retell the story.
2. Students can provide reasonable answers to the questions.

1. Read the Story ■

2. Go over the Story in Hevruta ■

3. Discuss the Questions ■

1. **What did the women figure out about what God wants from us?** God wants us to work together.

2. **What is the lesson of this midrash?** Cooperation is a way to work miracles.

3. **How can remembering the story of the women help us to point our hearts when we say the מִי כָמֹכָה?** By remembering that we worked together to get out of Egypt.

TRANSLATION/BIG READING

This page has students work on a translation on the response of מִי כָמֹכָה.

Big Ideas

1. Growing and reinforcing Hebrew vocabulary leads to a growing affinity with the liturgy.
2. Applying the Hebrew they have to form rough translations of Hebrew prayers (a) helps students to feel closer to those texts, (b) reinforces the Hebrew they are learning and (c) develops a process they can continue to apply to the Siddur.

Learning Activities

1. Introducing/reviewing vocabulary
2. Working out a trial translation
3. Correcting translations
4. Prayer drill
5. Rehearsal/performance

You Know You've Succeeded When...

1. Students work out a reasonable translation of this text.
2. Students correct their translation.
3. Students successfully perform these texts.

1. **Introducing/Reviewing Vocabulary** ■ [a] Using VOCABULARY POSTERS and FLASHCARDS, introduce and drill the core vocabulary needed for this translation. [b] Some game playing or team competition is the perfect way to reinforce this vocabulary.

2. **Working out a Trial Translation** ■ [a] Working in pairs, students should develop their own best TRANSLATION. [b] They should not worry about being perfect—they should worry about coming close. EXPECT a working translation something like:

   God is King for ever and ever.

3. **Correcting Translations** ■
   • יִמְלֹךְ is a verb (will rule)—not a noun.

4. **Prayer Drill** ■ Practice performing this portion of the prayer. SING or READ it together.

5. **Rehearsal/Performance** ■ Students work in *hevruta* pairs rehearsing the words and phrases on this page before performing them.

Saying כ with a Mouth Full of Water

H ere is another story of the first time that Israel said the מִי־כָמֹכָה. To understand this story you need to look at the words of the מִי־כָמֹכָה.

מִי־כָמֹכָה בָּאֵלִם יי, מִי כָּמֹכָה נֶאְדָּר בַּקֹּדֶשׁ, נוֹרָא תְהִלֹּת עֹשֵׂה פֶלֶא.

כָמֹכָה is spelled with a כ the first time. It is כָּמֹכָה with a כּ the second time. Israel entered the Reed Sea singing together. When they sang מִי, the water was up to their ankles. The word בָּאֵלִם came as they moved forward and the water reached their waists. By יי the water was at their chests. They were getting nervous, and so they sang more slowly. When they sang the second מִי, the water was up to their necks. Still they pushed on and tried to sing כָּמֹכָה. By the second כָמֹכָה, the water was over their heads. It came out as כָמֹכָה, because you can't say a כּ when your mouth is full of water. Only when they were in over their heads did God divide the sea. (From the Midrash)

Questions
1. What does this story teach us about what God expects from us?
2. What is the lesson of this midrash?
3. How can remembering the story of the water over our heads help us to point our hearts when we say the מִי־כָמֹכָה?

45

STORY: SAYING THE כ WITH A MOUTH FULL OF WATER

This third story is a another story of people being partners in the process of their redemption. God demands that we walk as far as we can before doing the Divine part of the miracle.

Big Ideas
1. We must do what we can on our own.
2. Redemption comes when we begin the process.

Learning Activities
1. Read the story
2. Go over the story in Hevruta
3. Discuss the questions

You Know You've Succeeded When...
1. Students can retell the story.
2. Students can provide reasonable answers to the questions.

1. Read the Story ■

2. Go over the Story in Hevruta ■

3. Discuss the Questions ■

1. **What does this story teach us about what God expects from us?** To do as much as we can on our own.

2. **What is the lesson of this midrash?** Redemption comes through our maximum efforts expanded by God's help.

3. **How can remembering the story of the water over our heads help us to point our hearts when we say the מִי כָמֹכָה?** It makes the מִי כָמֹכָה a song we sing as we march into the sea and not just a song we sing after the miracle. Your students may have many other creative suggestions

Blank Page

הַשְׁכִּיבֵנוּ

Lesson 12

Lesson 13

LESSON 12: הַשְׁכִּיבֵנוּ

These are the core concepts in this overview.

Big Ideas

1. The evening שְׁמַע and her blessings have an extra blessing that comes after the blessing after the שְׁמַע.
2. This blessing, the הַשְׁכִּיבֵנוּ, is added on as "part II" of the redemption blessing and has the added theme of asking God to protect us when we sleep.
3. This blessing has different endings for weekdays and Shabbat.

Learning Activities

1. Introducing the unit
2. Exploring the themes
3. Reviewing the key themes

You Know When You've Succeeded When ...

- Students can describe the structural position and themes of הַשְׁכִּיבֵנוּ.

1. Introducing the Unit ■ READ the introduction.

2. Exploring the Themes ■ CONVEY THE INFORMATION IN THE INTRODUCTION: Do one of the following. [a] DESCRIBE the information to your students. [b] READ out loud and DISCUSS this information or [c] ASSIGN your students to READ the information on their own and then DISCUSS it.

3. Reviewing the Key Themes ■

1. Review the structure of the בְּרָכוֹת that surround the שְׁמַע. They are creation, revelation, then the שְׁמַע, then redemption.
2. Review the themes of הַשְׁכִּיבֵנוּ: (a) as the extension of the redemption בְּרָכָה and (b) as a request for protection at night.

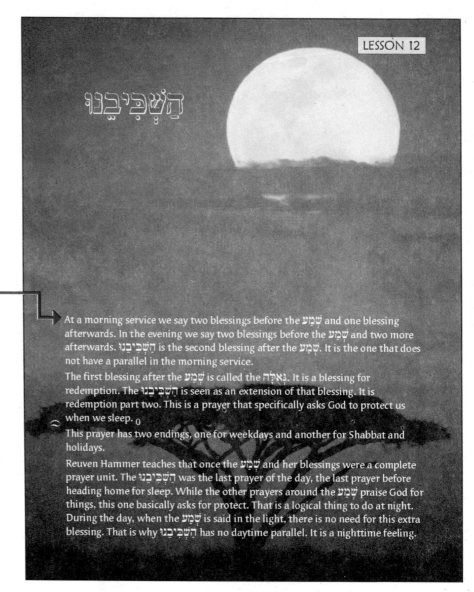

LESSON 12

At a morning service we say two blessings before the שְׁמַע and one blessing afterwards. In the evening we say two blessings before the שְׁמַע and two more afterwards. הַשְׁכִּיבֵנוּ is the second blessing after the שְׁמַע. It is the one that does not have a parallel in the morning service.

The first blessing after the שְׁמַע is called the גְּאֻלָה. It is a blessing for redemption. The הַשְׁכִּיבֵנוּ is seen as an extension of that blessing. It is redemption part two. This is a prayer that specifically asks God to protect us when we sleep.

This prayer has two endings, one for weekdays and another for Shabbat and holidays.

Reuven Hammer teaches that once the שְׁמַע and her blessings were a complete prayer unit. The הַשְׁכִּיבֵנוּ was the last prayer of the day, the last prayer before heading home for sleep. While the other prayers around the שְׁמַע praise God for things, this one basically asks for protect. That is a logical thing to do at night. During the day, when the שְׁמַע is said in the light, there is no need for this extra blessing. That is why הַשְׁכִּיבֵנוּ has no daytime parallel. It is a nighttime feeling.

46

הַשְׁכִּיבֵנוּ

Let us lie down in PEACE, ADONAI, our God,	הַשְׁכִּיבֵנוּ יי אֱלֹהֵינוּ לְשָׁלוֹם,	1.
and then let us stand back up alive, our Ruler,	וְהַעֲמִידֵנוּ מַלְכֵּנוּ לְחַיִּים,	2.
and spread over us a Sukkah of YOUR Peace	וּפְרוֹשׂ עָלֵינוּ סֻכַּת שְׁלוֹמֶךָ,	3.
and fix us with good advice before You	וְתַקְּנֵנוּ בְּעֵצָה טוֹבָה מִלְּפָנֶיךָ,	4.
and save us for Your own NAME's sake.	וְהוֹשִׁיעֵנוּ לְמַעַן שְׁמֶךָ.	5.
Protect us, Side with us, and turn away from us	וְהָגֵן בַּעֲדֵנוּ, וְהָסֵר מֵעָלֵינוּ	6.
ENEMIES, SICKNESS, the SWORD, HUNGER and SORROW	אוֹיֵב דֶּבֶר וְחֶרֶב וְרָעָב וְיָגוֹן,	7.
and turn away Satan from before us and from behind us	וְהָסֵר שָׂטָן מִלְּפָנֵינוּ וּמֵאַחֲרֵינוּ.	8.
and shelter us in the shadow of Your wings	וּבְצֵל כְּנָפֶיךָ תַּסְתִּירֵנוּ,	9.
Because You are God, The ONE Who guards and rescues us.	כִּי אֵל שׁוֹמְרֵנוּ וּמַצִּילֵנוּ אָתָּה,	10.
Because You are God, the Gracious and Merciful Ruler.	כִּי אֵל מֶלֶךְ חַנּוּן וְרַחוּם אָתָּה.	11.
the ONE Who guards us in our GOINGS and COMINGS	וּשְׁמוֹר צֵאתֵנוּ וּבוֹאֵנוּ	12.
in LIFE and in PEACE	לְחַיִּים וּלְשָׁלוֹם	13.
forever and always.	מֵעַתָּה וְעַד עוֹלָם.	14.
BLESSED be You, ADONAI	בָּרוּךְ אַתָּה יי	15.
The ONE Who spreads a Sukkah of Peace over us	הַפּוֹרֵשׂ סֻכַּת שָׁלוֹם עָלֵינוּ	16.
and over all of the nation Israel	וְעַל כָּל עַמּוֹ יִשְׂרָאֵל	17.
and on Jerusalem.	וְעַל יְרוּשָׁלָיִם.	18.

47

TEXT, TRANSLATION & COMMENTARY

The full הַשְׁכִּיבֵנוּ is presented for practice.

Big Ideas

1. When we enable students to perfect performances of core liturgy we make it possible for them to far more easily participate in communal worship.

2. By scanning the English of prayers students can grow insights into the meaning of the liturgy.

Learning Activities

1. Scanning the English text
2. Practicing the Hebrew text

You Know You've Succeeded When...

1. Students describe insights gained from looking at the English text.
2. Students practice their performance of the Hebrew text.
3. Students read, discuss and respond to the commentary.

1. Scanning the English Text ■ INVITE students to SCAN the English translation of these prayers. ASK them what "big ideas" they can find by looking. INSIGHTS that might be shared:

- This prayer is about protection.
- It is about protection during sleep.
- It is also about protection from big things like enemies and sickness.
- It closes with the image of a sukkah of peace.

2. Practicing the Hebrew Text ■ [a] INVITE students to work with a partner and practice the prayer. [b] READ or SING the prayers together as a class. [c] INVITE individual students or teams of students to perform individual lines or sections.

ROOTS שכב AND עמד

This page studies the roots שכב and עמד.

Big Ideas

1. Mastering Hebrew roots dramatically improves comprehension.
2. Looking at words built out of a single root enhances an understanding of Hebrew thinking.

Learning Activities

1. Analysis of the root שכב
2. Identifying words built out of שכב
3. Reading and identifying activity
4. Analysis of the root עמד
5. Identifying words built out of עמד
6. Reading and identifying activity

You Know You've Succeeded When...

1. Students can identify words with the שכב root.
2. Students can identify words with the עמד root.

1. Analysis of the Root שכב ■

a. Use the board or flashcards to introduce the root שכב and the words built out of it. The book uses no icon for שכב (because it is too abstract and might involve personifying God).

b. Establish the connection between the three words: שָׁכַב, שִׁכְבִי, הַשְׁכִּיבֵנוּ.

2. Identifying Words Built out of שכב ■

a. ASK: What word idea connects שָׁכַב, שִׁכְבִי, הַשְׁכִּיבֵנוּ?

b. ESTABLISH that "lie down" is the core idea.

3. Reading and Identifying Activity ■

a. Let students prepare these lines with a Hevruta partner.

b. Go over the passage. Invite individual students to read. Ask the entire class to read out together the words built out of the root שכב.

4. Analysis of the Root עמד ■

a. Use the board or flashcards to introduce the root עמד and the words built out of it.

b. Establish the connection between the three words: עוֹמֵד, עֲמִידָה, עַמּוּד.

5. Identifying Words Built out of עמד ■

a. ASK: What word idea connects עוֹמֵד, עֲמִידָה, עַמּוּד?

b. ESTABLISH that the connection here is "stand".

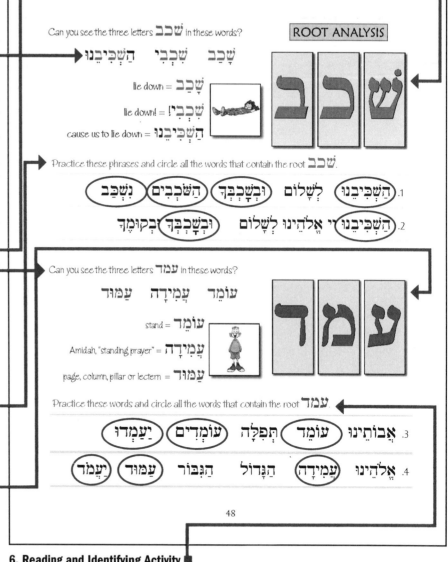

Can you see the three letters שכב in these words?

ROOT ANALYSIS

הַשְׁכִּיבֵנוּ   שִׁכְבִי   שָׁכַב

lie down = שָׁכַב

lie down! = שִׁכְבִי!

cause us to lie down = הַשְׁכִּיבֵנוּ

Practice these phrases and circle all the words that contain the root שכב.

1. הַשְׁכִּיבֵנוּ לְשָׁלוֹם וּבְשָׁכְבְּךָ הַשֹּׁכְבִים נִשְׁכַּב

2. הַשְׁכִּיבֵנוּ יְיָ אֱלֹהֵינוּ לְשָׁלוֹם וּבְשָׁכְבְּךָ וּבְקוּמֶךָ

Can you see the three letters עמד in these words?

עוֹמֵד   עֲמִידָה   עַמּוּד

stand = עוֹמֵד

Amidah, "standing prayer" = עֲמִידָה

page, column, pillar or lectern = עַמּוּד

Practice these words and circle all the words that contain the root עמד.

3. אֲבוֹתֵינוּ עוֹמֵד תְּפִלָּה עוֹמְדִים יַעֲמְדוּ

4. אֱלֹהֵינוּ עֲמִידָה הַגָּדוֹל הַגִּבּוֹר עַמּוּד יַעֲמֹד

48

6. Reading and Identifying Activity ■

a. Let students prepare these lines with a *hevruta* partner.

b. Go over the passage. Invite individual students to read. Ask the entire class to read out loud together the words built out of the root עמד.

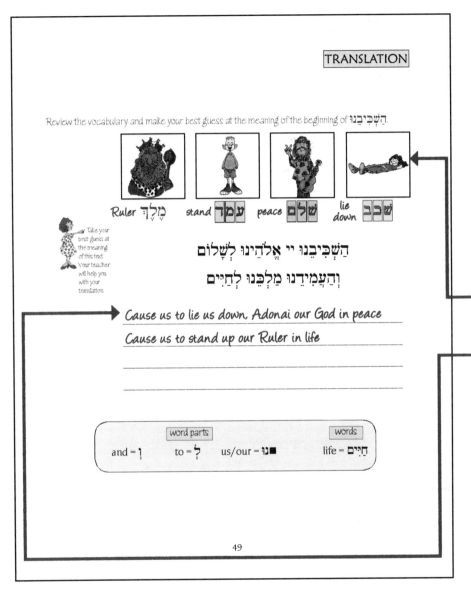

TRANSLATION

Review the vocabulary and make your best guess at the meaning of the beginning of הַשְׁכִּיבֵנוּ.

Ruler מֶלֶךְ   stand עֲמֹד   peace שָׁלוֹם   lie down שָׁכַב

☞ Take your best guess at the meaning of this text. Your teacher will help you with your translation.

הַשְׁכִּיבֵנוּ יי אֱלֹהֵינוּ לְשָׁלוֹם

וְהַעֲמִידֵנוּ מַלְכֵּנוּ לְחַיִּים

Cause us to lie us down, Adonai our God in peace

Cause us to stand up our Ruler in life

_____

_____

word parts		words
and = וְ to = לְ us/our = ◼נוּ		life = חַיִּים

49

TRANSLATION

This page has students work on a translation of the first line of הַשְׁכִּיבֵנוּ.

Big Ideas
1. Growing and reinforcing Hebrew vocabulary leads to a growing affinity with the liturgy.
2. Applying the Hebrew they have to form rough translations of Hebrew prayers (a) helps students to feel closer to those texts, (b) reinforces the Hebrew they are learning and (c) develops a process they can continue to apply to the Siddur.

Learning Activities
1. Introducing/reviewing vocabulary
2. Working out a trial translation
3. Correcting translations
4. Prayer drill

You Know You've Succeeded When...
1 Students work out a reasonable translation of this text.
2. Students correct their translation.
3. Students successfully perform these texts.

1. **Introducing/Reviewing Vocabulary** ◼ [a] Using VOCABULARY POSTERS and FLASHCARDS, introduce and drill the core vocabulary needed for this translation. [b] Some game playing or team competition is the perfect way to reinforce this vocabulary.

2. **Working out a Trial Translation** ◼ [a] Working in pairs, students should develop their own best TRANSLATION. [b] They should not worry about being perfect—they should worry about coming close. EXPECT a working translation something like:
   Lie us down Adonai our God to peace
   Stand us up our king to life

3. **Correcting Translations** ◼
   • הָעֲמִידֵנוּ and הַשְׁכִּיבֵנוּ are both in a grammatical construction called "הִפְעִיל" and can best be translated as "cause us to lie down" and "cause us to stand up."
   • the לְ in לְשָׁלוֹם and לְחַיִּים can best be understood as "in" and not "to."

4. **Prayer Drill** ◼ Practice performing this portion of the prayer. SING or READ it together.

LESSON 13: ROOT ANALYSIS

This page works on the root שלם, the theme word of these prayers.

Big Ideas

1. Mastering Hebrew roots dramatically improves comprehension.
2. Looking at words built out of a single root enhances an understanding of Hebrew thinking.
3. The Hebrew word שָׁלוֹם really means "whole" or "complete." The English word "peace" means "quiet" or "still."
4. Perception of roots in context builds both comprehension and connection.

Learning Activities

1. Analysis of the root שלם
2. Identifying words built out of שלם
3. Reading and identifying activity

You Know You've Succeeded When...

- Students can identify words with the שלם root.

1. Analysis of the Root שלם ■

a. Use the board or flashcards to introduce the root שלם and the words built out of it.

b. Establish the connection between the three words: שָׁלוֹם, שְׁלֵמָה, מְשַׁלֵם.

2. Identifying Words Built out of שלם ■

a. ASK: What word idea connects שָׁלוֹם, שְׁלֵמָה, מְשַׁלֵם?

b. ESTABLISH that the שלם root really means "whole" or "complete." Have students connect the meanings of the three words. Here is the key: The Jewish vision of peace has to do with "wholeness." Likewise, when one pays a bill, one is completing a transaction.

3. Reading and Identifying Activity ■

a. Let students prepare these lines with a Hevruta partner.

b. Go over the passage. Invite individual students to read. Ask the entire class to read out together the words built out of the root שלם.

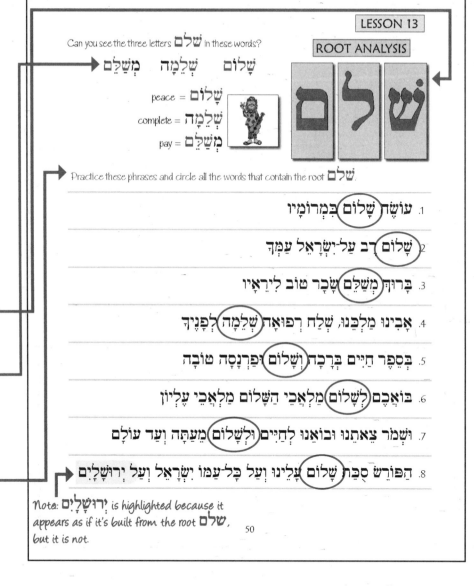

LESSON 13

ROOT ANALYSIS

שׁ ל ם

Can you see the three letters שלם in these words?

מְשַׁלֵם   שְׁלֵמָה   שָׁלוֹם

peace = שָׁלוֹם

complete = שְׁלֵמָה

pay = מְשַׁלֵם

Practice these phrases and circle all the words that contain the root שלם.

1. עוֹשֶׂה שָׁלוֹם בִּמְרוֹמָיו

2. שָׁלוֹם רָב עַל־יִשְׂרָאֵל עַמְּךָ

3. בָּרוּךְ מְשַׁלֵם שָׂכָר טוֹב לִירֵאָיו

4. אָבִינוּ מַלְכֵּנוּ, שְׁלַח רְפוּאָה שְׁלֵמָה לְפָנֶיךָ

5. בְּסֵפֶר חַיִּים בְּרָכָה וְשָׁלוֹם וּפַרְנָסָה טוֹבָה

6. בּוֹאֲכֶם לְשָׁלוֹם מַלְאֲכֵי הַשָּׁלוֹם מַלְאֲכֵי עֶלְיוֹן

7. וּשְׁמֹר צֵאתֵנוּ וּבוֹאֵנוּ לְחַיִּים וּלְשָׁלוֹם מֵעַתָּה וְעַד עוֹלָם

8. הַפּוֹרֵשׂ סֻכַּת שָׁלוֹם עָלֵינוּ וְעַל כָּל־עַמּוֹ יִשְׂרָאֵל וְעַל יְרוּשָׁלָיִם

Note: יְרוּשָׁלַיִם is highlighted because it appears as if it's built from the root שלם, but it is not.

50

50

TRANSLATION

Review the vocabulary and make your best guess at the meaning of the הַחֲתִימָה of הַשְׁכִּיבֵנוּ.

| peace שָׁלוֹם | סֻכָּה sukkah | פֹּרֵשׂ spreads | אַתָּה You | בָּרוּךְ bless |

Take your best guess at the meaning of this text. Your teacher will help you with your translation.

עַל on

יִשְׂרָאֵל Israel

יְרוּשָׁלַיִם Jerusalem

בָּרוּךְ אַתָּה יי הַפֹּורֵשׂ סֻכַּת שָׁלוֹם
עָלֵינוּ וְעַל כָּל-עַמּוֹ יִשְׂרָאֵל
וְעַל יְרוּשָׁלָיִם

Blessed are You Adonai the spreads sukkah peace

On us and on all His people Israel

And on Jerusalem

word parts		words
the = הַ	and = וְ / וּ	all = כָּל
us/our = ■נוּ	his = ו■	nation = עַם

51

TRANSLATION

This page has students work on the *hatimah* of הַשְׁכִּיבֵנוּ.

Big Ideas

1. Growing and reinforcing Hebrew vocabulary leads to a growing affinity with the liturgy.
2. Applying the Hebrew they have to form rough translations of Hebrew prayers (a) helps students to feel closer to those texts, (b) reinforces the Hebrew they are learning and (c) develops a process they can continue to apply to the Siddur.

Learning Activities

1. Introducing/reviewing vocabulary
2. Working out a trial translation
3. Correcting translations
4. Prayer drill

You Know You've Succeeded When...

1. Students work out a reasonable translation of this text.
2. Students correct their translation.
3. Students successfully perform these texts.

1. **Introducing/Reviewing Vocabulary** ■ [a] Using VOCABULARY POSTERS and FLASHCARDS, introduce and drill the core vocabulary needed for this translation. [b] Some game playing or team competition is the perfect way to reinforce this vocabulary.

2. **Working out a Trial Translation** ■ [a] Working in pairs, students should develop their own best TRANSLATION. [b] They should not worry about being perfect—they should worry about coming close. EXPECT a working translation something like:
   Blessed are You Adonai the spreads sukkah peace
   On us and on all His people Israel
   And on Jerusalem

3. **Correcting Translations** ■
   • הַפֹּורֵשׂ = the One Who spreads
   • סֻכַּת שָׁלוֹם = sukkat of peace (sukkat is סְמִיכוּת).

4. **Prayer Drill** ■ Practice performing this portion of the prayer. SING or READ it together.

STORY

A boy moves from slave to king with the help of a dream and a crystal.

Big Ideas

1. God protects people.
2. It is important to remember that we were slaves.
3. It is important to thank God for the blessings we receive.

Learning Activities

1. Read the story
2. Go over the story in Hevruta
3. Discuss the questions

You Know You've Succeeded When...

1. Students can retell the story.
2. Students can provide reasonable answers to the questions.

1. Read the Story ■

2. Go over the story in Hevruta ■

3. Discuss the Questions ■

1. **What do you think is the lesson that this story teaches?** There are a number of different lessons that can be learned from this story, including the three listed under Big Ideas on this page.

2. **Where do we find a crystal that lights the darkness for us?** This calls for a personal image. It may include "God," prayer, etc.

3. **How does knowing this story help you to point your heart when you say the הַשְׁכִּיבֵנוּ?** This is also a personal answer but will probably center on the idea of "protection."

The Bird of Happiness

There was a special light that shone when God created the world. It disappeared when Adam and Eve left the Garden. God took a piece of this light, put it in a crystal, and gave it to Adam and Eve to light the darkness. The crystal was passed from generation to generation. Noah used this crystal to light the inside of the Ark. It was passed from Abraham to Isaac to Jacob and made it to Solomon who used it to light the inside of the Temple. When the Temple was destroyed it disappeared.

Aaron was a Jewish boy. He and his family were escaped slaves walking through a desert. One night Aaron had a dream of being lost in a sand storm and being rescued by a large white bird. When he awoke he found a glowing crystal in his hand. He hung it from a leather thong around his neck. It only glowed when they were walking in the right direction. It led them to pools of water and oases filled with fruit. It led them to a great city that they learned was Jerusalem. They also learned that the king had died and the city needed a new one. To find the new kind they released the Bird of Happiness. When it landed on Aaron's shoulder, the boy who had been a slave became the new King. It was the bird of his dream.

The people dressed him in robes and put a crown on his head. His family now lived in a palace. The crystal became a guide. It would glow when the right answer was yes. It would remain dark if the right answer was no. One hour a day Aaron snuck away to a shack. He took off his royal garb and put on the rags he wore as a slave. He wanted to remember where he had come from. He also gave thanks every day for the blessings that the Bird of Happiness brought. *(Iraqi Jewish Folk Tale)*

Questions

1. What do you think is the lesson that this story teaches?
2. Where do we find a crystal that lights the darkness for us?
3. How does knowing this story help you to point your heart when you say the הַשְׁכִּיבֵנוּ?

52

וְשָׁמְרוּ

The next lessons deal with the וְשָׁמְרוּ. This lesson is made up of (a) an introduction, (b) the text of וְשָׁמְרוּ, (c) a midrashic origin story for Shabbat and (d) the translation of the first part of this prayer.

Lesson 14

Page 53: We meet וְשָׁמְרוּ as a biblical text that also introduces the idea of "an extra soul."

Page 54: Next we consider the Hebrew and English text of וְשָׁמְרוּ.

Page 55: We continue by looking at two key roots, שבת and נפש.

Page 56: A translation of the second half of the prayer follows.

Page 57: We end the lesson by studying a story that connects Shabbat to the extra soul.

Blank Page

The Shabbat commandment was read in the middle of this prayer. But in a period of time when *some* people began to believe that the Ten Commandments were the only important part of the Torah, the Rabbis made a switch. In the evening service they used the וַיְכֻלּוּ, a piece of Torah that comes from the Shabbat part of the story of creation (*Gen.* 2.1-3). On Saturday morning they used the וְשָׁמְרוּ (*Ex.* 31.16-17), which is a lesson about Shabbat that Moses taught soon after the incident of the Golden Calf.

LESSON 14: וְשָׁמְרוּ

These are the core concepts in this overview.

Big Idea

1. וְשָׁמְרוּ is from the Torah.
2. וְשָׁמְרוּ is used in a number of different ways over Shabbat.
3. וְשָׁמְרוּ is the source for the idea that we get "an extra soul" over Shabbat.

Learning Activities

1. Introducing the unit
2. Exploring the themes
3. Reviewing the key themes

You Know You've Succeeded When...

1. Students can restate that וְשָׁמְרוּ is from the Torah.
2. Students can restate that וְשָׁמְרוּ is used in a number of different ways over Shabbat.
3. Students can restate that וְשָׁמְרוּ is the source for the idea that we get "an extra soul" over Shabbat.

1. Introducing the Unit ■ READ the introduction.

2. Exploring the Themes ■ CONVEY THE INFORMATION IN THE INTRODUCTION: Do one of the following. [a] DESCRIBE the information to your students. [b] READ out loud and DISCUSS this information. [c] ASSIGN your students to READ the information on their own and then DISCUSS it.

a. Read the English text of the וְשָׁמְרוּ on page 54. Establish the source as coming from Exodus 31.16-17.

b. Explore the concept of "an extra soul" on Shabbat. Show how the words שָׁבַת וַיִּנָּפַשׁ can mean both "did Shabbat and rested" and "observed Shabbat and resouled."

3. Reviewing the Key Themes ■

These are the core concepts:

1. וְשָׁמְרוּ is from the Torah.
2. וְשָׁמְרוּ is used in a number of different ways over Shabbat.
3. וְשָׁמְרוּ is the source for the idea that we get "an extra soul" over Shabbat.

TEXT, TRANSLATION & COMMENTARY

The full text of וְשָׁמְרוּ is presented.

Big Ideas

1. When we enable students to perfect performances of core liturgy we make it possible for them to far more easily participate in communal worship.

2. By scanning the English of prayers students can grow insights into the meaning of the liturgy.

Learning Activities

1. Scanning the English text
2. Practicing the Hebrew text

You Know You've Succeeded When...

1 Students describe insights gained from looking at the English text.
2. Students practice their performance of the Hebrew text.
3. Students read, discuss and respond to the commentary.

1. Scanning the English Text ■ INVITE students to SCAN the English translation of these prayers. ASK them what "big ideas" they can find by looking. INSIGHTS that might be shared:

- Just as God rested on Shabbat, we rest on Shabbat.
- Shabbat is part of our covenant with God.
- Shabbat can help us "re-soul."

2. Practicing the Hebrew Text ■ [a] INVITE students to work with a partner and practice the prayer. [b] READ or SING the prayers together as a class. [c] INVITE individual students or teams of students to perform individual lines or sections.

וְשָׁמְרוּ

The Families-of-Israel shall KEEP SHABBAT	1. וְשָׁמְרוּ בְנֵי־יִשְׂרָאֵל אֶת־הַשַּׁבָּת
to MAKE SHABBAT	2. לַעֲשׂוֹת אֶת־הַשַּׁבָּת
in every generation as a forever COVENANT.	3. לְדֹרֹתָם בְּרִית עוֹלָם.
Between Me and the Families-of-Israel	4. בֵּינִי וּבֵין בְּנֵי יִשְׂרָאֵל
SHABBAT is a forever sign.	5. אוֹת הִיא לְעֹלָם
Because in six days ADONAI MADE	6. כִּי־שֵׁשֶׁת יָמִים עָשָׂה יי
heavens and earth,	7. אֶת־הַשָּׁמַיִם וְאֶת־הָאָרֶץ
but on The Seventh Day	8. וּבַיּוֹם הַשְּׁבִיעִי
God had a SHABBAT and re-SOULED.	9. שָׁבַת וַיִּנָּפַשׁ.

54

ROOTS נפש AND שבת

This page studies the roots שבת and נפש.

Big Ideas

1. Mastering Hebrew roots dramatically improves comprehension.
2. Looking at words built out of a single root enhances an understanding of Hebrew thinking.

Learning Activities

1. Analysis of the root שבת
2. Identifying words built out of שבת
3. Reading and identifying activity
4. Analysis of the root נפש
5. Identifying words built out of נפש
6. Reading and identifying activity

You Know You've Succeeded When...

1. Students can identify words with the שבת root.
2. Students can identify words with the נפש root.

1. Analysis of the Root שבת ▪

a. Use the board or flashcards to introduce the root שבת and the words built out of it. The book uses no icon for שבת (because it is too abstract and might involve personifying God).

b. Establish the connection between the three words: שַׁבָּת, יִשְׁבַּת, שָׁבַת.

2. Identifying Words Built out of שבת ▪

a. ASK: What word idea connects שַׁבָּת, יִשְׁבַּת, שָׁבַת?

b. ESTABLISH that "lie down" is the core idea.

3. Reading and Identifying Activity ▪

a. Let students prepare these lines with a Hevruta partner.

b. Go over the passage. Invite individual students to read. Ask the entire class to read out together the words built out of the root שבת.

4. Analysis of the Root נפש ▪

a. Use the board or flashcards to introduce the root נפש and the words built out of it.

b. Establish the connection between the three words: נֶפֶשׁ, נַפְשְׁךָ, וַיִּנָּפַשׁ.

5. Identifying Words Built out of נפש ▪

a. ASK: What word idea connects נֶפֶשׁ, נַפְשְׁךָ, וַיִּנָּפַשׁ?

b. ESTABLISH that the connection here is "stand".

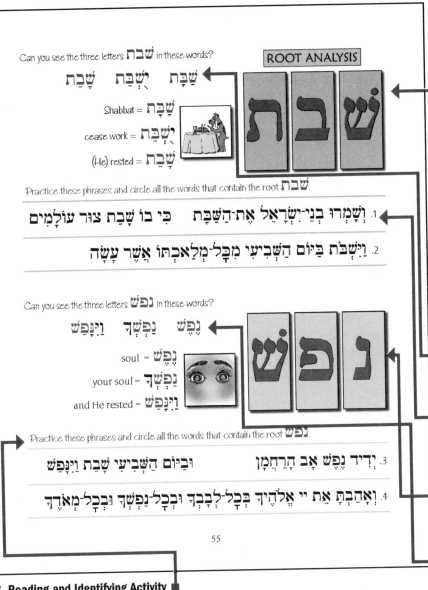

ROOT ANALYSIS

Can you see the three letters שבת in these words?

שָׁבַת יִשְׁבַּת שַׁבָּת

Shabbat = שַׁבָּת

cease work = יִשְׁבַּת

(He) rested = שָׁבַת

Practice these phrases and circle all the words that contain the root שבת.

1. וְשָׁמְרוּ בְנֵי־יִשְׂרָאֵל אֶת־הַשַּׁבָּת   כִּי בוֹ שָׁבַת צוּר עוֹלָמִים

2. וַיִּשְׁבֹּת בַּיּוֹם הַשְּׁבִיעִי מִכָּל־מְלַאכְתּוֹ אֲשֶׁר עָשָׂה

Can you see the three letters נפש in these words?

וַיִּנָּפַשׁ נַפְשְׁךָ נֶפֶשׁ

soul = נֶפֶשׁ

your soul = נַפְשְׁךָ

and He rested = וַיִּנָּפַשׁ

Practice these phrases and circle all the words that contain the root נפש.

3. יְדִיד נֶפֶשׁ אָב הָרַחֲמָן   וּבַיּוֹם הַשְּׁבִיעִי שָׁבַת וַיִּנָּפַשׁ

4. וְאָהַבְתָּ אֵת יי אֱלֹהֶיךָ בְּכָל־לְבָבְךָ וּבְכָל־נַפְשְׁךָ וּבְכָל־מְאֹדֶךָ

55

6. Reading and Identifying Activity ▪

a. Let students prepare these lines with a Hevruta partner.

b. Go over the passage. Invite individual students to read. Ask the entire class to read out loud together the words built out of the root נפש.

TRANSLATION

On this page we are going to translate the second half of the וְשָׁמְרוּ and study the word וַיִּנָּפַשׁ to learn about "the extra soul" we get on Shabbat.

Big Ideas

1. Growing and reinforcing Hebrew vocabulary leads to a growing affinity with the liturgy.
2. Applying the Hebrew they have to form rough translations of Hebrew prayers (a) helps students to feel closer to those texts, (b) reinforces the Hebrew they are learning and (c) develops a process they can continue to apply to the Siddur.

Learning Activities

1. Introducing/reviewing vocabulary
2. Working out a trial translation
3. Correcting translations
4. Prayer drill

You Know You've Succeeded When...

1. Students work out a reasonable translation of this text.
2. Students correct their translation.

1. Introducing/Reviewing Vocabulary ■ [a] Using VOCABULARY POSTERS and FLASHCARDS, introduce and drill the core vocabulary needed for this translation. [b] Some game playing or team competition is the perfect way to reinforce this vocabulary.

2. Working out a Trial Translation ■ [a] Working in pairs, students should develop their own best TRANSLATION. [b] They should not worry about being perfect—they should worry about coming close. EXPECT a working translation something like:

That (in) six days made Adonai
The heavens and the earth
And in the day the seven rested and re-souled.

3. Correcting Translations ■

a. Figuring out to add the "in" in the first line.

b. In the third line understanding the בְּ as "on" and not "in" will be helpful.

c. Explaining that "יוֹם הַשְּׁבִיעִי" is "the seventh day" may be useful.

4. Prayer Drill ■ Practice performing this portion of the prayer. SING or READ it together.

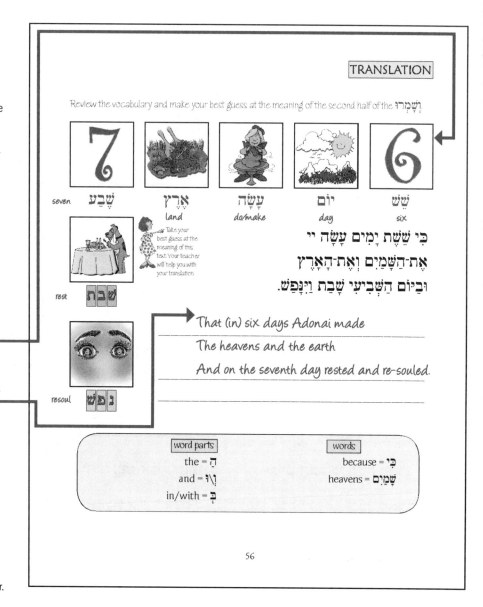

In the beginning, God was alone. So God created the angels, the other heavenly creatures, and people, too. The first thing God created was light. It was a special kind of light—one that came directly from God. On the fourth day of creation God created the sun, the moon, and the stars. The original light was hidden away.

On the first Shabbat God stopped working and gathered all of Creation. The angel of Shabbat got to sit on the throne of glory, and all of the angels got to rest. They gathered round and folded their six wings. On the seventh day they could not sing. God brought Adam and Eve up to heaven to join in the Shabbat celebration. They were the ones who began to sing, "It is good to give thanks to God," the words that later started the Shabbat psalm. The angels joined in.

God told Adam and Eve that a piece of the Garden of Eden is in every Shabbat. God said, "During Shabbat you will be able to taste the world to come." God then decided that a little bit of the original hidden light would be released into the world every Shabbat. (Assembled through the notes in Louis Ginzberg's *Legends of the Jews*).

Questions
1. What is the special connection between Shabbat and people?
2. How does Shabbat connect us to God?
3. How can knowing this story help us to point our hearts when we say קְרוּשַׁת הַיּוֹם in the עֲמִידָה on

57

STORY: THE FIRST SHABBAT

This story connects Shabbat to creation and also builds a connection to a unique spiritual presence that is perceivable on Shabbat.

Big Ideas

1. God created people so that they could praise God in an honest way. Angels have no free will and have to praise God.

2. Shabbat has a unique spiritual character. We describe it as having a spark of "hidden light," a portion of the "Garden of Eden," and a foretaste of the "World to Come." This is another way of talking about the "extra soul" feeling.

Learning Activities

1. Read the story
2. Go over the story in Hevruta
3. Discuss the questions

You Know You've Succeeded When...

1. Students can retell the story.
2. Student can provide reasonable answers to the questions.

1. Read the Story ■

2. Go over the Story in Hevruta ■

3. Discuss the Questions ■

1. **What is the special connection between Shabbat and people?** *Students may offer answers that are connected to the story or they may come from their own experience. So you may get* "People rest on Shabbat." "People light Shabbat candles." *They may give answers they have learned, like* "God gave people Shabbat as a gift" *or* "God ordered us to keep Shabbat." *Those are all good answers, but the answer that comes out of the story is* "People were the ones who realized how good resting on Shabbat was and thanked God for the gift."

2. **How does Shabbat connect us to God?** *Some good answers you can expect are:* "God gave us Shabbat." "We rest on Shabbat just like God did." *Or even* "When we rest on Shabbat and don't work we can feel closer to God." *This story suggests and you may want to add,* "There is something special, a hidden light, a piece of the Garden of Eden or an extra soul" *that we can feel on Shabbat.*

3. **How can knowing this story help us to point our heart when we say וְשָׁמְרוּ on Shabbat?** *The answer we might hope for is* "We can look for the hidden light—we can find a Garden-of-Eden-like peace."

Blank Page

אָבוֹת וְאִמָּהוֹת

With this lesson we begin our study of the אָבוֹת וְאִמָּהוֹת.

Lesson 15

Page 58: We begin with an overview of this בְּרָכָה that inclues the context, the midrashic context and the importance of this בְּרָכָה as a place to balance the role of women in the Jewish tradition.

Page 59: Next we present the entire prayer and its English translation. This page (20) will be an ongoing resource through this unit.

Page 60: Finally, we translate the opening phrases of this בְּרָכָה. This is the part of the prayer that deals with individual God relationships. (As part of this page we also look at the choreography that happens during this phrase.)

Lesson 16

Page 61: The study of two key roots—[חסד] and [זכר].

Page 62: The translation of another key phrase from the אָבוֹת וְאִמָּהוֹת, the one that contains חַסְדֵי אָבוֹת, and additional "decoding practice".

Page 63: Next we translate the phrase about God being מֶלֶךְ עוֹזֵר וּמוֹשִׁיעַ וּמָגֵן. We read and discuss the story *Abraham Was a Hero*.

Page 64: Finally we study a story that features Abraham's missing mother.

LESSON 15: INTRODUCTION

With this lesson we are now into the heart of the book. This page serves as the introduction to the אָבוֹת וְאִמָּהוֹת.

Big Ideas

1. Knowing the position of a prayer in the structure of a service helps us to understand its purpose and meaning.

2. The central idea of this בְּרָכָה is זְכוּת אָבוֹת (the merit of the ancestors). It teaches the double-sided idea that (a) we use our family connections to ask God for help and (b) by learning from our family history we become the kind of people God wants.

3. The story of Moses getting God to forgive Israel after the Golden Calf is one of the foundational "origin" stories for this prayer. It again attaches the עֲמִידָה to repentance and forgiveness.

4. The אָבוֹת וְאִמָּהוֹת is one of the locations where the challenge of including women as coequal participants in the Jewish tradition has been played out. In this day and age we have a mandate to tell the story of Jewish women as effectively and as expansively as we have told the story of Jewish men.

Learning Activities

1. Introducing the unit
2. Exploring the themes
3. Reviewing the key themes

You Know You've Succeeded When...

1. Students can describe the theme of the אָבוֹת וְאִמָּהוֹת.
2. Students can state the connection of the prayer to Moses.

1. Introducing the Unit ■ Among the good ways of introducing the unit are (a) lecture-discussion, (b) students reading the page in order to answer some key questions you provide or (c) discussing one portion of the introduction each session.

2. Exploring the Themes ■ CONVEY THE INFORMATION IN THE INTRODUCTION: Do one of the following. [a] DESCRIBE the information to your students. [b] READ out loud and DISCUSS this information. [c] ASSIGN your students to READ the information on their own and then DISCUSS it.

1. The אָבוֹת וְאִמָּהוֹת is the first בְּרָכָה in the עֲמִידָה. It is the first of three praise בְּרָכוֹת.

2. It is rooted in the idea of זְכוּת אָבוֹת.

3. One of the "origin stories" involves Moses' prayers to God after the sin of the Golden Calf.

אָבוֹת וְאִמָּהוֹת

The אָבוֹת וְאִמָּהוֹת is the first prayer in the עֲמִידָה. Rabbi Simlai taught in the Talmud, "One must always start the עֲמִידָה with praise of God before one asks anything of God" (*Brakhot* 32a).

• The אָבוֹת וְאִמָּהוֹת is the first of three "praise" בְּרָכוֹת that begin the עֲמִידָה.

• The big idea of this prayer is זְכוּת אָבוֹת (the merit of our ancestors). This means that we ask God to take care of us because our ancestors were good people who had good relationships with God.

• The Rabbis who organized the סִדּוּר explained their choice of the אָבוֹת וְאִמָּהוֹת as the first prayer because of a Torah story about Moses.

Originally, this prayer was just about the אָבוֹת, the "fathers," אַבְרָהָם, יִצְחָק, and יַעֲקֹב. Like many things in Judaism, it was "man" centered. Today many synagogues have added the אִמָּהוֹת, the mothers, שָׂרָה, רִבְקָה, לֵאָה and רָחֵל. This came as part of a growing understanding that all of us need women's stories, too.

4. The original אָבוֹת has invited the addition of the אִמָּהוֹת in recent years. It is a perfect example of the ongoing growth of the Judaism tradition.

3. Reviewing the Key Themes ■

אָבוֹת וְאִמָּהוֹת

Blessed be You, ADONAI	1. בָּרוּךְ אַתָּה יי
our God and God of our FATHERS & our MOTHERS	2. אֱלֹהֵינוּ וֵאלֹהֵי אֲבוֹתֵינוּ וְאִמּוֹתֵינוּ.
God of ABRAHAM	3. אֱלֹהֵי אַבְרָהָם
God of ISAAC	4. אֱלֹהֵי יִצְחָק
and God of JACOB	5. וֵאלֹהֵי יַעֲקֹב.
God of SARAH	6. אֱלֹהֵי שָׂרָה
God of REBEKKAH	7. אֱלֹהֵי רִבְקָה
God of LEAH	8. אֱלֹהֵי רָחֵל
and God of RACHEL	9. וֵאלֹהֵי לֵאָה.
The GOD, The GREAT One, The HERO, THE AWESOME One	10. הָאֵל הַגָּדוֹל הַגִּבּוֹר וְהַנּוֹרָא
God on High	11. אֵל עֶלְיוֹן
The ONE-Who-NURSES with GOOD KINDNESS	12. גּוֹמֵל חֲסָדִים טוֹבִים
and the ONE-Who-OWNS everything	13. וְקוֹנֵה הַכֹּל
and the ONE-Who-REMEMBERS the kindness of the Parents,	14. וְזוֹכֵר חַסְדֵי אָבוֹת וְאִמָּהוֹת
and brings a REDEMEER/REDEMPTION	15. וּמֵבִיא גוֹאֵל/גְּאוּלָה
to their children's children	16. לִבְנֵי בְנֵיהֶם
for the sake of God's NAME.	17. לְמַעַן שְׁמוֹ בְּאַהֲבָה.
RULER, HELPER—and SAVIOR and PROTECTOR.	18. מֶלֶךְ עוֹזֵר וּמוֹשִׁיעַ וּמָגֵן.
Blessed be You, ADONAI	19. בָּרוּךְ אַתָּה יי
The ONE-Who-PROTECTS Abraham	20. מָגֵן אַבְרָהָם
and The ONE-Who HELPS Sarah/REMEMBERS Sarah.	21. וְעֶזְרַת שָׂרָה/וּפֹקֵד שָׂרָה.

*Traditional version   *Reform and Reconstructionist version

59

TRANSLATION AND TEXT

This page contains the Hebrew and English text of the אָבוֹת וְאִמָּהוֹת. It should be used for both introducing the prayer and practicing and perfecting its performance.

Big Ideas

1. When we enable students to perfect performances of the core liturgy we make it possible for them to far more easily participate in communal worship.

2. By scanning the English of prayers students can grow insights into the meaning of the liturgy.

3. The אָבוֹת וְאִמָּהוֹת is a prayer with many versions at the moment that reflect ideological diversity between various movements and subgroupings.

Learning Activities

1. Scanning the English text
2. Practicing the Hebrew text

You Know You've Succeeded When...

1 Students describe insights gained from looking at the English text.
2. Students practice their performance of the Hebrew text.

1. Scanning the English Text ■ INVITE students to SCAN the English translation of these prayers. ASK them what "big ideas" they can find by looking. Look at the differences in the liturgical formulae.

2. Practicing the Hebrew Text ■ [a] INVITE students to work with a partner and practice the prayer. [b] READ or SING the prayers together as a class. [c] INVITE individual students or teams of students to perform individual lines or sections.

TRANSLATION

This page combines two things: (1) a translation of the first verse of the אָבוֹת וְאִמָהוֹת and (2) a look at the choreography of the prayer.

Big Ideas

1. Growing and reinforcing Hebrew vocabulary leads to a growing affinity with the liturgy.
2. Applying the Hebrew they have to form rough translations of Hebrew prayers (a) helps students to feel closer to those texts, (b) reinforces the Hebrew they are learning and (c) develops a process they can continue to apply to the Siddur.
3. Choreography of the בָּרְכוּ

Learning Activities

1. Introducing/reviewing vocabulary
2. Working out a trial translation
3. Correcting translations
4. Prayer drill
5. Discussing choreography

You Know You've Succeeded When...

1. Students work out a reasonable translation of this text.
2. Students correct their translation.
3. Students unpack the choreography of the אָבוֹת וְאִמָהוֹת.

Translation

1. Introducing/Reviewing Vocabulary ■ [a] Using VOCABULARY POSTERS and FLASHCARDS, introduce and drill the core vocabulary needed for this translation. [b] Some game playing or team competition is the perfect way to reinforce this vocabulary.

2. Working out a Trial Translation ■ [a] Working in pairs, students should develop their own best TRANSLATION. [b] They should not worry about being perfect—they should worry about coming close. EXPECT a working translation something like:

Bless You Adonai our God and God of our fathers and mothers
God of Abraham, God of Isaac and God of Jacob
God of Sarah, God of Rebekkah, God of Leah and God of Rahel.

3. Correcting Translations ■ The only "improvement" you may want to add is that "אֱלֹהֵי" means *the God of...* If you know enough Hebrew grammar to understand *"smikhut,"* then it will be easy to explain. If you don't know that much grammar, it is not that important (so don't worry about it).

4. Prayer Drill ■ Practice performing this portion of the prayer. SING or READ it together.

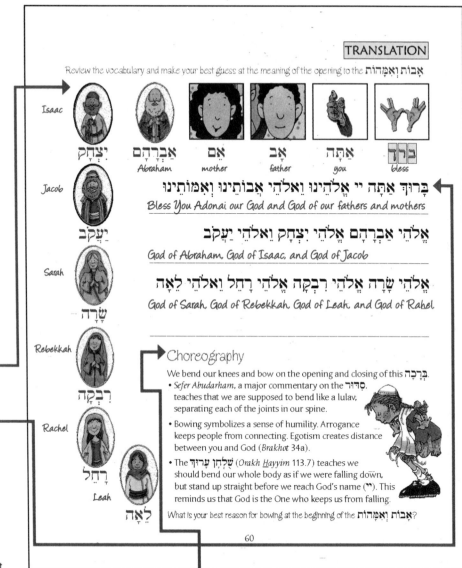

TRANSLATION

Review the vocabulary and make your best guess at the meaning of the opening to the אָבוֹת וְאִמָהוֹת

Isaac — יִצְחָק | Abraham — אַבְרָהָם | mother — אֵם | father — אָב | you — אַתָּה | bless — ברך

בָּרוּךְ אַתָּה יי אֱלֹהֵינוּ וֵאלֹהֵי אֲבוֹתֵינוּ וְאִמוֹתֵינוּ
Bless You Adonai our God and God of our fathers and mothers

אֱלֹהֵי אַבְרָהָם אֱלֹהֵי יִצְחָק וֵאלֹהֵי יַעֲקֹב
God of Abraham, God of Isaac, and God of Jacob

אֱלֹהֵי שָׂרָה אֱלֹהֵי רִבְקָה אֱלֹהֵי רָחֵל וֵאלֹהֵי לֵאָה
God of Sarah, God of Rebekkah, God of Leah, and God of Rahel

Jacob — יַעֲקֹב | Sarah — שָׂרָה | Rebekkah — רִבְקָה | Rachel — רָחֵל | Leah — לֵאָה

Choreography

We bend our knees and bow on the opening and closing of this בְּרָכָה.

- *Sefer Abudarham*, a major commentary on the סִדוּר, teaches that we are supposed to bend like a lulav, separating each of the joints in our spine.

- Bowing symbolizes a sense of humility. Arrogance keeps people from connecting. Egotism creates distance between you and God (*Brakhot* 34a).

- The שֻׁלְחָן עָרוּךְ (*Orakh Hayyim* 113.7) teaches we should bend our whole body as if we were falling down, but stand up straight before we reach God's name (יי). This reminds us that God is the One who keeps us from falling.

What is your best reason for bowing at the beginning of the אָבוֹת וְאִמָהוֹת?

60

5. Discussing the Choreography ■

1. Have students stand up and practice the "knee bend bow."

2. Let students read the three explanations of bowing, and then invite them to pick the one they like best. By having advocates for the three explanations you can go over all of this material from the student perspective.

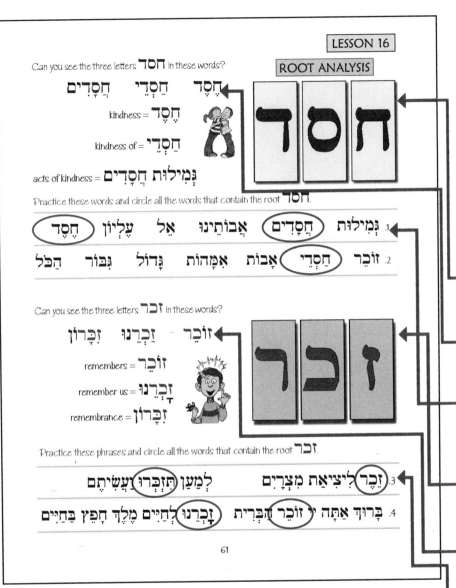

LESSON 16: TWO ROOTS

This page studies the roots חסד and זכר.

Big Ideas

1. Mastering Hebrew roots dramatically improves comprehension.
2. Looking at words built out of a single root enhances an understanding of Hebrew thinking.

Learning Activities

1. Analysis of the root חסד
2. Identifying words built out of חסד
3. Reading and identifying activity
4. Analysis of the root זכר
5. Identifying words built out of זכר
6. Reading and identifying activity

You Know You've Succeeded When...

1. Students can identify words with the חסד root.
2. Students can identify words with the זכר root.

1. Analysis of the Root חסד
a. Use the board or flashcards to introduce the root חסד and the words built out of it..
b. Establish the connection between the three words: חֶסֶד, חַסְדֵי, גְּמִילוּת חֲסָדִים.

2. Identifying Words Built out of חסד
a. ASK: What word idea connects חֶסֶד, חַסְדֵי, גְּמִילוּת חֲסָדִים?
b. ESTABLISH that "kindness" is the core idea.

3. Reading and Identifying Activity
a. Let students prepare these lines with a Hevruta partner.
b. Go over the passage. Invite individual students to read. Ask the entire class to read out together the words built out of the root חסד.

4. Analysis of the Root זכר
a. Use the board or flashcards to introduce the root זכר and the words built out of it.
b. Establish the connection between the three words: זוֹכֵר, זָכְרֵנוּ, זִכָּרוֹן.

5. Identifying Words Built out of זכר
a. ASK: What word idea connects זוֹכֵר, זָכְרֵנוּ, זִכָּרוֹן?
b. ESTABLISH that "remember" is the core idea.

6. Reading and Identifying Activity
a. Let students prepare these lines with a hevruta partner.

b. Go over the passage. Invite individual students to read. Ask the entire class to read out loud together the words built out of the root זכר.

TRANSLATION/PRACTICE

This page contains both the chance to work on translating a key phrase from the בְּרָכָה and more "decoding" drill. While this phrase doesn't specifically use the words זְכוּת אָבוֹת, it is the place where this value is rooted.

Big Ideas

1. Growing and reinforcing Hebrew vocabulary leads to a growing affinity with the liturgy.
2. Applying the Hebrew they have to form rough translations of Hebrew prayers (a) helps students to feel closer to those texts, (b) reinforces the Hebrew they are learning and (c) develops a process they can continue to apply to the Siddur.

Learning Activities

1. Introducing/reviewing vocabulary
2. Working out a trial translation
3. Correcting translations
4. Prayer drill
5. Practice text

You Know You've Succeeded When...

1. Students work out a reasonable translation of this text.
2. Students correct their translation.

1. Introducing/Reviewing Vocabulary ■ [a] Using VOCABULARY POSTERS and FLASHCARDS, introduce and drill the core vocabulary needed for this translation. [b] Some game playing or team competition is the perfect way to reinforce this vocabulary.

2. Working out a Trial Translation ■ [a] Working in pairs, students should develop their own best TRANSLATION. [b] They should not worry about being perfect—they should worry about coming close. EXPECT a working translation something like:
And remember kindness of fathers and mothers.

3. Correcting Translations ■

Help students by pointing out that חַסְדֵי means "kindness of." The י ending here replaces the Hebrew word שֶׁל and means "of."

4. Prayer Drill ■ Practice performing this portion of the prayer. SING or READ it together.

5. Practice Text ■ Work out a way for students to get the maximum amount of practicing and the least amount of unfocused waiting time while you use this drill opportunity. Here are a few suggestions.
- mass reading where lots of people read at once
- small group work where students get a chance to read a lot more
- random reading patterns (not necessarily at the end of individual lines) where students have to be on their toes to participate
- use of technology, tape recordings and the like

TRANSLATION

Review the vocabulary and make your best guess at the meaning of another part of the אָבוֹת וְאִמָהוֹת.

come/bring בוא · אם mother · אב father · חסד kindness · זכר remember

children בָּנִים

love אהב

Your teacher will help you with your translation.

וְזוֹכֵר חַסְדֵי אָבוֹת וְאִמָהוֹת
וּמֵבִיא גוֹאֵל/גְאוּלָה לִבְנֵי בְנֵיהֶם
לְמַעַן שְׁמוֹ בְּאַהֲבָה

And remember the kindness of the fathers and mothers.

_____

_____

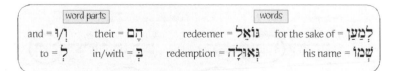

word parts			words	
and = וְ/וּ	their = הֶם	redeemer = גוֹאֵל	for the sake of = לְמַעַן
to = לְ	in/with = בְּ	redemption = גְאוּלָה	his name = שְׁמוֹ

62

3. How can knowing this story help you know where to point your heart when you say the וְאִמָהוֹת אָבוֹת? We can look for moments when we have had experiences like this one—when we found the strength to do something that was hard, when we found ourselves safe when we never expected to get through something but we found a way. These are moments when we may realize that God has been our shield. To help you understand this you may want to use the joke about the flood.

Review the vocabulary and make your best guess at the meaning of another part of the אָבוֹת וְאִמָּהוֹת.

 TRANSLATION

Your teacher will help you with your translation.

word parts	words
and = וְ	help = עוֹזֵר
	save = מוֹשִׁיעַ

Ruler מֶלֶךְ   shield מָגֵן

מֶלֶךְ עוֹזֵר וּמוֹשִׁיעַ וּמָגֵן.

Ruler, helper, and savior and shield

Abraham Was a Hero

A war was going on in Canaan. It had nothing to do with Abraham. Four local kings were fighting five other local kings. Abraham (who was still Abram) was camped in the trees at Mamre when a refugee from the war staggered into camp. The refugee told him that Abraham's nephew Lot, who lived in Sodom, had been taken prisoner. The four kings had raided Sodom and Gomorrah, robbed all the wealth, and then run away. Abraham gathered an army from the people in his camp. He chased the four kings into the north of Canaan. His army caught them and defeated them. Abraham rescued Lot and gathered up all of the possessions that had been stolen. He returned everything to the original owners. He kept nothing for himself. He gave nothing to his army. Melchizedek, king of Salem, threw a party. He gave Abraham (still Abram) a blessing. He said, "Blessed be Abram of אֵל עֶלְיוֹן, Creator of heaven and earth." Abraham then blessed God with words that would later become part of the Psalms: "You, God, are a shield about me...I have no fear of the many forces that surround me" (Ps. 3.4-7). At that moment the angels in heaven started to sing, "בָּרוּךְ אַתָּה יי מָגֵן אַבְרָהָם" (Gen. 14.; P.R.E. 27).

Questions

1. What are the things we learn about Abraham that make him into a hero?
2. What connections do we find between this story and the אָבוֹת וְאִמָּהוֹת?
3. How can knowing this story help you know where to point your heart when you say the אָבוֹת וְאִמָּהוֹת?

63

The second connection involves Abram not taking anything for himself out of the spoils. These are the insights you may want to add: (a) Abram not taking anything for himself was an act of חֶסֶד—one of those "role model" things we should try to emulate. (b) God might have been Abram's shield in that Abram's loyalty to God's values helped to keep him from being greedy when he won the battle. God protected Abram from his worst possible self. continued on page 62

TRANSLATION/STORY

This page allows students to translate another small fragment of the אָבוֹת וְאִמָּהוֹת and looks at a story of Abraham.

Big Ideas

1. Growing and reinforcing Hebrew vocabulary leads to an affinity with the liturgy.
2. Applying the Hebrew they have to form rough translations of Hebrew prayers (a) helps students to feel closer to those texts, (b) reinforces the Hebrew they are learning and (c) develops a process they can continue to apply.
3. The stories of Abraham's experience of being shielded and saved by God allow us to find moments when we can experience the same forces in our own lives.

Learning Activities

1. Introducing/reviewing vocabulary
2. Working out a trial translation
3. Correcting translations
4. Prayer drill
5. Reading the story

You Know You've Succeeded When...

1. Students work out a reasonable translation of this text.
2. Students correct their translation.
3. Students unpack the story "Abraham was a Hero".

1. Introducing/Reviewing Vocabulary ■ [a] Using VOCABULARY POSTERS and FLASHCARDS, introduce and drill the core vocabulary needed for this translation. [b] Some game playing or team competition is the perfect way to reinforce this vocabulary.

2. Working out a Trial Translation ■ [a] Working in pairs, students should develop their own best TRANSLATION. [b] They should not worry about being perfect—they should worry about coming close. EXPECT a working translation something like:
Ruler, helper, and savior and shield

3. Correcting Translations ■ Help students by pointing out that חַסְדֵי means "kindness of." The י ending here replaces the Hebrew word שֶׁל and means "of."

4. Prayer Drill ■ Practice performing this portion of the prayer. SING or READ it together.

5. Reading the Story ■ Read, tell or have students read the story in small groups. Discuss the questions.

1. **What are the things we learn about Abraham that make him into a hero?** (a) He wins a great battle against all odds. (b) He rescues people. (c) He shows incredible honesty, keeping none of the spoils of battle for himself.

2. **What connections do we find between this story and the אָבוֹת וְאִמָּהוֹת?** There are two connections. One is obvious and one is more subtle. The obvious one you can expect your students to get: One of the reasons that Abram was able to succeed in battle was because God protected him. When Abraham realized this and thanked God for being his "Shield," the אָבוֹת וְאִמָּהוֹת was said for the first time.

THE MISSING MOTHER—A BONUS STORY

The "missing mother" is a collection of stories about Abram's mother Amat'la-i who is found in the midrash but not in the biblical text. This story shows that (a) she was a monotheist before her son, and (b) she directed his future by becoming his first student.

Big Ideas

1. The midrash often provides us with stories we are seeking that cannot be found in the biblical text.
2. Even with moments of human weakness, we can still act like heroes.
3. Great people have parents and mentors who often propel them toward their accomplishments.

Learning Activities

1. Read the story
2. Go over the story in Hevruta
3. Discuss the questions

You Know You've Succeeded When...

1. Students can retell the story.
2. Students can provide reasonable answers to the questions.

1. Read the Story ■

2. Go over the Story in Hevruta ■

3. Discuss the Questions ■

1. **In what ways was Amat'la-i a great role model? All Jews (even Jews-by-choice) are children of Abraham. That makes her your "grandmother." In what ways would you like to be like her?** *Your students will suggest some of these; you will want to fill in those they don't get:* (a) She stands up to king and husband to protect her child, (b) She is the first monotheist with real faith in prayer, (c) She overcomes the guilt of having abandoned her child and comes back and (d) She empowers Abram's teaching by becoming his first student.

2. **The hard thing about this story is knowing that Amat'la-i left her newborn baby alone in a cave. How can you understand that?** *Your students may well be able to say, "She was scared." "She didn't know what to do." "She trusted God to take care of him."*

   Those are all good answers—and there are no better, other than to explain that sometimes people "overload" when things are too chaotic—they freeze. "The great part of this story is that she came back."

The Missing Mother (A Bonus Story)

Abraham's mother was called Amat'la-i, the daughter of Karnibo, but you can't find her story in the Torah. You have to look for her in the Talmud and the Midrash.

Nimrod was the wicked king who built the tower of Babel. Like all wicked kings he wanted people to believe that he was a god. Nimrod learned from an astrologer that soon a male child would be born who would grow up and teach everyone that Nimrod was not a god. That did not make Nimrod happy. He ordered the midwives of his empire to make sure that all male babies died. At the same time he offered a prize for every girl that was born. Nimrod built a huge palace and made all of the pregnant women in his realm live there. He pretended to take care of them, but this gave him a chance to make sure that no boys survived.

Amat'la-i was married to Terah, the idol maker. He was a member of Nimrod's court. Amat'la-i hid the fact that she was pregnant. She knew that if Terah knew, he would turn her in. When it was time for her to give birth she went out to the wilderness. Abram (who would become Abraham) was born in a cave. His mother blessed him with three blessings: "May God be with you. May God never fail you. May God never leave you." Then she left him.

Here is where the miracles start. Baby Abram sucked his thumb, and out came milk. This milk was amazing food. Ten days after his birth Abram was big enough and strong enough to stand up and walk out of the cave. He looked at the world and the way that nature works. He became the first person to figure out that One God had created everything. He prayed to that One God, saying, "I believe in You." Then, for the first time, he heard God's voice saying, "And I believe in you."

Amat'la-i felt sick about having abandoned her child. She ran back to the cave and found it empty. While she was sitting at its entrance sobbing, a child, not a newborn, came up to her and said, "Why are you crying?" She explained, and he said, "Mother, don't you recognize me?" She hugged him, and he explained to her about the One God. Abraham's mother, the one who risked her life to give him life, became his first student (Based on Louis Ginzberg, *The Legends of the Jews*).

Questions

1. In what ways was Amat'la-i a great role model? All Jews (even Jews-by-choice) are children of Abraham. That makes her your "grandmother." In what ways would you like to be like her?

2. The hard thing about this story is knowing that Amat'la-i left her newborn baby alone in a cave. How can you understand that?

3. How can knowing the story of Abraham's mother help you point your heart when you pray the אָבוֹת וְאִמָהוֹת?

64

---

3. **How can knowing the story of Abraham's mother help you point your heart when you pray the אָבוֹת וְאִמָהוֹת?** Once again, we have a woman whose life we can imitate.

גְּבוּרוֹת

This unit is about the גְּבוּרוֹת.

Lesson 17

Page 65: The גְּבוּרוֹת introduction gives the setting, theme and biblical source for this prayer.

Page 66: Next we have two editions of the Hebrew/English text of the prayer. One is the traditional, the other is the Reform. These pages come with commentaries and can be reused each lesson.

Page 67: We begin by translating and comparing the traditional, Reform and Reconstructionist opening lines to the גְּבוּרוֹת, using this as an opportunity to discuss the different beliefs reflected in the three versions.

Lesson 18

Page 68: This lesson begins with a "decoding" drill that includes phrases from the גְּבוּרוֹת.

Page 69: We translate another piece of the גְּבוּרוֹת that includes God's acts of loving kindness.

Page 70-71: Finally, we read a midrash about Joseph that shows how he is the "poster child" for גְּמִילוּת חֲסָדִים.

Blank Page

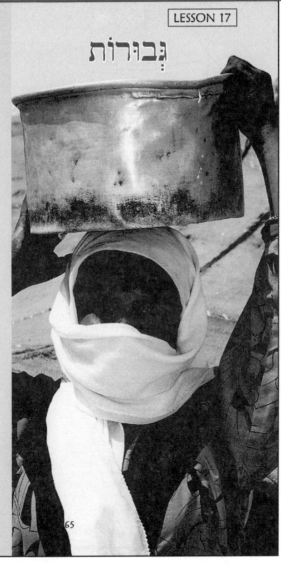

The גְּבוּרוֹת is:
- the second of the three praise בְּרָכוֹת that begin the עֲמִידָה.
- called the גְּבוּרוֹת (the "power" prayer) (*Megillah* 17b). That makes it a prayer that talks about God's power through describing some of the good things that God does for people.
- also called מְחַיֵּה הַמֵּתִים (The One-Who-Gives-Life-to-the-Dead) (*Brakhot* 33a). It is a prayer that traditionally centers on the idea that God is stronger than death.

The גְּבוּרוֹת is a place where some modern Jews have changed the סִדּוּר. In a number of סִדּוּרִים the phrase מְחַיֵּה הַמֵּתִים is replaced by מְחַיֵּה הַכֹּל (The One-Who-Gives-Life-to-All), or מְחַיֵּה כָּל חַי (The One Who-Gives-and-Renews Life).

In the same way that the אָבוֹת וְאִמָּהוֹת, the first prayer in the עֲמִידָה, tells the story of אַבְרָהָם and שָׂרָה and their experiences of God, the גְּבוּרוֹת grows out of stories of יִצְחָק and רִבְקָה.

65

- Reform Jews have changed these words because they reject the idea of resurrection of the dead.
- From this prayer we learn ways that we are supposed to be like God.

LESSON 17: גְּבוּרוֹת

This page anchors the גְּבוּרוֹת as the second בְּרָכָה in the עֲמִידָה, one of the praise בְּרָכוֹת, which praises God for doing mighty things including giving life after death.

Big Ideas
1. The גְּבוּרוֹת has two names; each name teaches us something about its meaning. גְּבוּרוֹת speaks of how God uses power to help us. מְחַיֵּה הַמֵּתִים teaches that God is "stronger than death."
2. Some Jews choose to change the words to prayers with which they disagree. Some Jews work hard to reunderstand them in ways they can accept. And some Jews believe that we have an obligation to believe certain traditional ideas—even if they are hard to accept.
3. When we praise God for doing great things we have an obligation to imitate those things.

Learning Activities
1. Introducing the unit
2. Exploring the themes
3. Reviewing the key themes

You Know You've Succeeded When...
1. Students can describe the location, names and themes in the גְּבוּרוֹת.
2. Students can explain why so many movements have changed the text of the גְּבוּרוֹת.
3. Students can list some of the things about God described in the גְּבוּרוֹת.

1. Introducing the Unit ■ Look at the English text on page 57. Have students suggest their "no more than four-word" theme for this prayer. Write the themes on the board. Then turn back to page 56 and read the text on that page.

2. Exploring the Themes ■ CONVEY THE INFORMATION IN THE INTRODUCTION: Do one of the following. [a] DESCRIBE the information to your students. [b] READ out loud and DISCUSS this information. [c] ASSIGN your students to READ the information on their own and then DISCUSS it.

3. Reviewing the Key Themes ■
- This is the second of three praise בְּרָכוֹת that begin the עֲמִידָה.
- It has two names, גְּבוּרוֹת (God's Power) and מְחַיֵּה הַמֵּתִים (God is stronger than Death). Each name teaches a lesson.

TRANSLATION AND TEXT

This page contains the Hebrew and English text of the גְּבוּרוֹת. It should be used both for introducing the prayer and for practicing and perfecting its performance.

Big Ideas

1. When we enable students to perfect performances of the core liturgy we make it possible for them to far more easily participate in communal worship.
2. By scanning the English of prayers students can grow insights into the meaning of the liturgy.
3. The אָבוֹת וְאִמָּהוֹת is a prayer with many versions at the moment that reflect ideological diversity between various movements and subgroupings.

Learning Activities

1. Scanning the English text
2. Practicing the Hebrew text
3. Examining the inserts

You Know You've Succeeded When...

1. Students describe insights gained from looking at the English text.
2. Students practice their performance of the Hebrew text.

1. Scanning the English Text ■ INVITE students to SCAN the English translation of these prayers. ASK them what "big ideas" they can find by looking. Look at the differences in the liturgical formulae.

2. Practicing the Hebrew Text ■ [a] INVITE students to work with a partner and practice the prayer. [b] READ or SING the prayers together as a class. [c] INVITE individual students or teams of students to perform individual lines or sections.

2. Examining the Inserts ■ The text between lines 3 and 4 is an insert into the גְּבוּרוֹת. It is a request for rain that is said between Sukkot (the fall harvest) and Passover (the spring harvest).

גְּבוּרוֹת

You are a HERO forever, my Master.	1. אַתָּה גִּבּוֹר לְעוֹלָם אֲדֹנָי
You give LIFE to the dead	2. מְחַיֵּה מֵתִים אַתָּה
You give LIFE to all	מְחַיֵּה הַכֹּל אַתָּה
You are GREAT to bring SALVATION.	3. רַב לְהוֹשִׁיעַ.
The ONE-Who-Returns the wind and Makes the rain come down.	מַשִּׁיב הָרוּחַ וּמוֹרִיד הַגֶּשֶׁם.
Cultivating LIFE in kindness	4. מְכַלְכֵּל חַיִּים בְּחֶסֶד
Giving LIFE to the dead/.	6. מְחַיֵּה מֵתִים/הַכֹּל/כָּל חַי
Giving LIFE to the dead with much mercy.	7. בְּרַחֲמִים רַבִּים.
The ONE-Who-LIFTS-UP the fallen	8. סוֹמֵךְ נוֹפְלִים
and HEALS the sick	9. וְרוֹפֵא חוֹלִים
and FREES prisoners	10. וּמַתִּיר אֲסוּרִים
and ESTABLISHES God's faith	11. וּמְקַיֵּם אֱמוּנָתוֹ
with those who sleep in the dust.	12. לִישֵׁנֵי עָפָר.
Who is like You, Master of Strength?	13. מִי כָמוֹךְ בַּעַל גְּבוּרוֹת?
And who has Your Image?	14. וּמִי דוֹמֶה לָּךְ?
RULER of DEATH and LIFE	15. מֶלֶךְ מֵמִית וּמְחַיֶּה
and the ONE-Who-Plants SALVATION.	16. וּמַצְמִיחַ יְשׁוּעָה.
And You are faithful to give LIFE to the dead.	17. וְנֶאֱמָן אַתָּה לְהַחֲיוֹת מֵתִים.
Blessed be You, ADONAI.	18. בָּרוּךְ אַתָּה יי
The One-Who-Gives LIFE to the dead.	19. מְחַיֵּה הַמֵּתִים/הַכֹּל/כָּל חַי.

Traditional/Reform/Reconstructionist

66

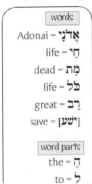

Review the vocabulary and make your best guess at the meaning of the opening of the גְּבוּרוֹת.

TRANSLATION

words

Adonai = אֲדֹנָי

life = חַי

dead = מֵת

life = כֹּל

great = רַב

save = [יְשַׁע]

word parts

the = הַ

to = לְ

עוֹלָם Cosmos/ forever
גִּבּוֹר strong/ hero
אַתָּה You

אַתָּה גִּבּוֹר לְעוֹלָם אֲדֹנָי

You are mighty to the world Adonai

You give life to the dead _____ אַתָּה מֵתִים מְחַיֵּה

You give life to all מְחַיֵּה הַכֹּל אַתָּה

You are great to bring salvation _____ רַב לְהוֹשִׁיעַ

Background on the Different Versions

תְּחִיַּת הַמֵּתִים (Resurrection of the Dead) is a belief that at some time in the future God will regather our bodies from the soil and place our souls back in them, giving us a second chance to live.

1. Maimonides was a famous Jewish philosopher who wrote a list of thirteen things that every Jew was supposed to believe. Number thirteen has to do with the phrase מְחַיֵּה הַמֵּתִים—giving life to the dead. "I believe with complete faith that there will be a resurrection of the dead whenever the Creator wishes it...For Your salvation, Eternal, do I wait."

2. In 1869 a conference of Reform rabbis voted on a resolution and decided "The belief in bodily resurrection has no religious foundation and the doctrine of immortality refers to the afterexistence of the soul alone." The Reform Movement adopted מְחַיֵּה הַכֹּל—giving life to all. Some services in recent Reform סִדּוּרִים have gone back to the original.

3. The Conservative Movement has left the words unchanged but often suggests different understandings. In a book called *Higher and Higher*, Steven M. Brown provides a list of alternative understandings: • People live on in the memories of others. • People's good works live on after them. • The soul is resurrected and comes back in another body. • People can be revived spiritually so life takes on new meaning. • People recuperate after severe illness. • Someone pronounced dead can be revived by C.P.R.

67

4. Prayer Drill ■ Practice performing this portion of the prayer. SING or READ it together.

5. Discussing Commentary ■ Ask students to identify the difference between the Reform and the traditional versions and identify the one used in your synagogue. The answer is "the One-Who-gives-life to the dead" versus "the One-Who-gives-Life to all."

TRANSLATION/COMMENTARY

This page combines two things: (a) Translations of the Reform and the traditional beginning of the גְּבוּרוֹת and (b) the idea of resurrection .

Big Ideas

1. Growing and reinforcing Hebrew vocabulary leads to an affinity with the liturgy.
2. Applying the Hebrew they have to form rough translations of Hebrew prayers (a) helps students to feel closer to those texts, (b) reinforces the Hebrew they are learning and (c) develops a process they can continue to apply to the Siddur.
3. Performance and comprehension of prayers are built through mastery of small elements.
4. Understanding resurrection of the dead.

Learning Activities

1. Introducing/reviewing vocabulary
2. Working out a trial translation
3. Correcting translations
4. Prayer drill
5. Discussing commentary

You Know You've Succeeded When...

1 Students work out a reasonable translation of this text.
2. Students correct their translation.
3. Students can discuss the different understandings of resurrection of the dead.

1. Introducing/Reviewing Vocabulary ■ [a] Using VOCABULARY POSTERS and FLASHCARDS, introduce and drill the core vocabulary needed for this translation. [b] Some game playing or team competition is the perfect way to reinforce this vocabulary.

2. Working out a Trial Translation ■ [a] Working in pairs, students should develop their own best TRANSLATION. [b] They should not worry about being perfect—they should worry about coming close. EXPECT a working translation something like:

> **You are mighty to the world Adonai—living dead—you are great to save.** Or maybe "**you are a rabbi who saves**" (the word רַב is misunderstood).
>
> **You are mighty to the world Adonai—living the all—you are great to save.**

3. Correcting Translations ■

(a) לְעוֹלָם here means "always" (sort of "You fill the cosmos in both time and space").

(b) Probably not worth mentioning, but here אֲדֹנָי means "My Master" and is not God's name being replaced with the word אֲדֹנָי.

(c) "מְחַיֵּה" means "the One-Who-gives-life," so one phrase is "the One-Who-gives-life to the dead," and the other is "the One-Who-gives-Life to all." (The "הַ" in Hebrew just doesn't translate into English.)

(d) רַב לְהוֹשִׁיעַ doesn't really translate easily into English. It sort of means "You are great because you offer us (the possibility) of salvation."

LESSON 18: BIG READING

This page has students practice phrases from the גְּבוּרוֹת.

Big Ideas

- Practice is good.

Learning Activities

1. Rehearsal/Performance
2. Phrase detective

You Know You've Succeeded When...

- Students successfully perform these texts.

1. **Rehearsal/Performance** ■ Students work in Hevruta pairs rehearsing the words and phrases on this page before performing them.

2. **Phrase Detective** ■

1. Invite students to look at these four phrases from the גְּבוּרוֹת and see what things they can find that they all share.

2. Listen to their answers. If they get that all have some form of מְחַיֵה הַמֵּתִים, great. If not, do the next two steps.

3. Set them looking for the root חַי in each phrase.

4. Set them looking for the word מֵת in each phrase.

5. End by saying, "חַי means life. מֵת means dead. Next time we will figure out how these two words go together to form the core of a major theme in this prayer."

Practice these phrases from the גְּבוּרוֹת.

1. וּמְקַיֵּם אֱמוּנָתוֹ לִישֵׁנֵי עָפָר   מְחַיֵּה הַכֹּל בְּרַחֲמִים רַבִּים

2. מִי כָמוֹךָ בַּעַל גְּבוּרוֹת   מְחַיֵּה כָל חַי

3. מֶלֶךְ מֵמִית וּמְחַיֶּה   וּמַצְמִיחַ יְשׁוּעָה   וּמִי דוֹמֶה לָּךְ

4. סוֹמֵךְ נוֹפְלִים   וְרוֹפֵא חוֹלִים   וּמַתִּיר אֲסוּרִים

5. מְכַלְכֵּל חַיִּים בְּחֶסֶד   מְחַיֵּה הַכֹּל בְּרַחֲמִים רַבִּים

6. אַתָּה גִבּוֹר לְעוֹלָם אֲדֹנָי   מְחַיֵּה מֵתִים אַתָּה רַב לְהוֹשִׁיעַ

7. וְנֶאֱמָן אַתָּה לְהַחֲיוֹת הַכֹּל   בָּרוּךְ אַתָּה יי מְחַיֵּה הַמֵּתִים

Phrase Detective

Look at these four phrases from the גְּבוּרוֹת. What do all four phrases have in common?

Answer: All the prases have words built from the root חי (life).

8. אַתָּה גִבּוֹר לְעוֹלָם אֲדֹנָי מְחַיֵּה מֵתִים אַתָּה רַב לְהוֹשִׁיעַ

9. מְכַלְכֵּל חַיִּים בְּחֶסֶד מְחַיֵּה כָל חַי בְּרַחֲמִים רַבִּים

10. מֶלֶךְ מֵמִית וּמְחַיֶּה וּמַצְמִיחַ יְשׁוּעָה

11. וְנֶאֱמָן אַתָּה לְהַחֲיוֹת מֵתִים בָּרוּךְ אַתָּה יי מְחַיֵּה הַכֹּל

68

TRANSLATION

Review the vocabulary and make your best guess at the meaning of this part of the גְּבוּרוֹת

| prisoner אָסוּר | sick חוֹלֶה | doctor/ רוֹפֵא heal | fall נוֹפֵל | lifts up סוֹמֵךְ |

 Take your best guess at the meaning of this text. Your teacher will help you with your translation.

sleep יָשֵׁן

סוֹמֵךְ נוֹפְלִים וְרוֹפֵא חוֹלִים וּמַתִּיר אֲסוּרִים
וּמְקַיֵּם אֱמוּנָתוֹ לִישֵׁנֵי עָפָר

Lifts up fall, heals sick, frees prisoners, and establishes
God's faith with sleepers in the dust.

dust עָפָר

---

words

free = מַתִּיר   establish = מְקַיֵּם   God's faith = אֱמוּנָתוֹ

69

TRANSLATION

This page begins this lesson by having students (a) translate a phrase from the גְּבוּרוֹת and then (b) use them to learn about the concept of גְּמִילוּת חֲסָדִים (acts of loving kindness). We learn that we need to provide for other people's needs in the same way that God provides for our needs.

Big Ideas

1. God provides the source of help that we need (either directly or indirectly). This includes things like lifting up the fallen, healing the sick, freeing prisoners, etc.
2. We are obligated to do for others the same kinds of acts of kindness that God does for us.

Learning Activities

1. Introducing/reviewing vocabulary
2. Working out a trial translation
3. Correcting translations
4. Prayer drill

You Know You've Succeeded When...

1. Students work out a reasonable translation of this text.
2. Students correct their translation.

1. Introducing/Reviewing Vocabulary ■ [a] Using VOCABULARY POSTERS and FLASHCARDS, introduce and drill the core vocabulary needed for this translation. [b] Some game playing or team competition is the perfect way to reinforce this vocabulary.

2. Working out a Trial Translation ■ [a] Working in pairs, students should develop their own best TRANSLATION. [b] They should not worry about being perfect—they should worry about coming close. EXPECT a working translation something like:

Lifts up fall, heals sick, frees prisoners and establishes God's faith with sleepers in the dust.

3. Correcting Translations ■

- סוֹמֵךְ נוֹפְלִים = "lifts up THE fallen." This is a grammatical form called *smikhut* in which the "the" is implied.
- וּמְקַיֵּם אֱמוּנָתוֹ will be successfully translated as "keeping faith" but will need to be explained as "established a relationship of trust" (people learned that they could trust God).
- לִישֵׁנֵי עָפָר will be translated as "sleeps in the dust" but will need to be explained as either (a) the poor or (b) the dead (who will be resurrected—if you believe that).

4. Prayer Drill ■ Practice performing this portion of the prayer. SING or READ it together.

Joseph is the "poster child" for righteousness and גְּמִילוּת חֲסָדִים (as is Rebekkah). The "story" here is a collection of midrashim that show some examples of this.

Big Ideas

- The גְּבוּרוֹת teaches us to be a lot like Joseph and Rebekkah because they did many of the same acts of גְּמִילוּת חֲסָדִים that God does for us.
- The story of Joseph shows that one can emerge from difficult circumstances as a righteous person.
- The "feeling," "belief" or "knowledge" that God is with us can motivate and inspire our lives.

Learning Activities

1. Read the story
2. Go over the story in Hevruta
3. Discuss the questions

You Know You've Succeeded When...

1. Students can retell the story.
2. Students can provide reasonable answers to the questions.

1. Read the Story ◼ Tell, read or have students read the story. Before you move into the questions, have the students list "the good things" that Joseph did.

Here is a starting list.

1. To obey his father he went out to the pasture when it was dangerous for him.

2. He refused Potiphar's wife.

3. He was good to people in jail (not exactly in our story).

4. He made sure that food was available to all at fair prices.

5. He was good to the people seeking food.

6. He made up with his brothers and forgave them.

2. Go over the Story in Hevruta ◼

Joseph the Tzaddik

This story began with a father who favored one son over his other sons. Joseph, the favorite son, had dreams in which everyone bowed down to him. He was a kid who said "me" all the time. His brothers hated him for his dreams and for his special treatment.

One day, Jacob, their father, asked Joseph to go out to the pasture where the other brothers were watching the sheep. Joseph happily agreed. Maybe he didn't realize how much his brothers hated him. Maybe he didn't believe that anything bad could happen to him. Or maybe he just wanted to make his father happy. Whatever the reason, it was a trip that changed Joseph's life—and his whole family's life.

Joseph's brothers captured him, threw him in a pit, told his father that he was dead, and sold him as a slave. Joseph wound up in Potiphar's house in Egypt. There Joseph became responsible. He cared about doing a good job. Joseph became a very successful head of Potiphar's household. The problem came when Potiphar's wife

70

wanted to cheat on her husband with Joseph. They could have gotten away with it. But Joseph refused her saying, "I have to be loyal to my master." The midrash says, "He was ready to cheat but he saw his father's face."

Even though he said, "No," Joseph wound up in jail. There he made a point of learning the language of everyone else in jail. The Torah makes a point of telling us "God was with Joseph in jail." The midrash explains that Joseph lived with the knowledge that there was one God who demanded that people act with justice and kindness. Joseph became a leader in jail, too.

In jail Joseph explained some dreams. This got him the chance to explain Pharaoh's dreams. These dreams wound up meaning "Seven years of plenty and then seven years of famine." Joseph wound up in charge of Egypt, and everyone loved him. They bowed down to him, just like in his childhood dreams.

When the famine came, Joseph made sure that there was food for everyone—no favoritism. There was food for every Egyptian and food for strangers from other countries who came in need. Joseph could have charged oodles of money for the food, but he was fair and just in his pricing. The midrash tells us that he personally went and spoke to everyone who needed food in their own language—using the languages he learned in jail.

When his brothers came down to Egypt Joseph had the power to get even with them. Instead of revenge, he did two things. First, he helped them understand what they had done that was wrong. This understanding was a gift. Then he made sure that his family had food, safety, and a good place to live. He forgave and helped them. In the tradition, Joseph, the kid who started out saying, "me" all the time—was called יוֹסֵף הַצַּדִיק, Joseph the Righteous Person (*Various midrashim*).

Questions

1. Why did the Rabbis of the Talmud think that Joseph was a צַדִיק?
2. How did living with the knowledge that "God was with him" affect Joseph?
3. How can knowing the story of the kid who started out saying "me" all the time—who turned into יוֹסֵף הַצַּדִיק—help us to know where to point our hearts when we say the גְּבוּרוֹת?

71

3. Discuss the Questions

1. **Why did the rabbis of the Talmud think that Joseph was a צַדִיק?** *Your students will be able to list many or all of the things that we did on the previous page. But you will want to add,* "He was someone who started out being selfish (or seeming selfish), went through some really hard times, yet still emerged as a kind, caring person. Most exceptional is the fact that he forgave his brothers, who almost killed him. He did not turn bitter and angry—he turned kind."

2. **How did living with the knowledge that "God was with him" affect Joseph?** *The perfect answer would be* "He made a point of doing for others the things that God did for him." *Don't expect it. Expect:* "It gave him hope, strength, courage, etc." "It kept him from giving up." "It helped him explain dreams."

3. **How can knowing the story of the kid who started out saying "Me" all the time who turned into Joseph הַצַּדִיק help us to know where to point our hearts when we say the גְּבוּרוֹת?** *Here is our core answer:* "When we say the גְּבוּרוֹת we want to be like Joseph (and Rebekkah), knowing that "God is with us" and doing for others what God does for us." *Your students may have other wonderful answers because the question is pretty open ended. Expect answers like* "It can remind us that God will be with us the way that God was with Joseph." "We can go through hard times like Joseph and not turn bitter."

Blank Page

קְדוּשָׁה

This lesson has elements that provide an overview to the קְדוּשָׁה.

Lesson 19

LESSON 19: INTRODUCTION

This page provides the chance to introduce this unit and deals with the (a) location, (b) process of public worship (c) sources and (d) thematic foundation of the קְדוּשָׁה.

Big Ideas

- The location and role of the קְדוּשָׁה, the third בְּרָכָה in the עֲמִידָה, the last of the praise בְּרָכוֹת, teach us about its use. When we know the location and purpose of a בְּרָכָה, it empowers us to use it in a meaningful way.

- There are many different ways that different congregations pray the קְדוּשָׁה.

- קְדוֹשׁ הַשֵּׁם, the idea that we can make God's holiness seem more real with our holy actions, is a core Jewish value. We learn that we become holy through the doing of holy things.

Learning Activities

1. Introducing the unit
2. Exploring the themes
3. Reviewing the key themes

You Know You've Succeeded When...

1. Students can connect the קְדוּשָׁה to angels.
2. Students can describe the sources and location of the קְדוּשָׁה.
3. Students can explain "Making God's name holy."

1. Introducing the Unit ■ Ask each student to give a definition of "holiness" without using the word "special."

2. Exploring the Themes ■ CONVEY THE INFORMATION IN THE INTRODUCTION: Do one of the following. [a] DESCRIBE the information to your students. [b] READ out loud and DISCUSS this information. [c] ASSIGN your students to READ the information on their own and then DISCUSS it.

3. Reviewing the Key Themes ■

Tell, read or let students silently read the material. Here are the major points.

1. The קְדוּשָׁה is understood to be a collection of angels' prayers. (Angels can be metaphors.) We will find its origins in the stories of Isaiah, Ezekiel and Jacob.

2. The קְדוּשָׁה is the third בְּרָכָה in the עֲמִידָה, the last of the praise בְּרָכוֹת, and its theme is holiness.

3. קְדוּשָׁה is said differently in different congregations. It is important to point out the way your congregation does it.

4. There is a core Jewish value called קְדוֹשׁ הַשֵּׁם that challenges us act in holy ways both to make ourselves holy and to model and advertise God's holiness.

קְדוּשָׁה

The קְדוּשָׁה is understood to be the angels' prayer. For some Jews, angels are very real. For other Jews angels are a metaphor—a way of describing a special state of holiness, a special sense of closeness to God.

The קְדוּשָׁה is built out of stories about Isaiah, Ezekiel, and Jacob.

The קְדוּשָׁה is:

- the third praise בְּרָכָה that begins the עֲמִידָה.

- said silently in some congregations and then sometimes repeated aloud. In other settings it is only said aloud by the congregation.

- a dialogue, a back-and-forth singing or reading, between the congregation and the service leader.

- a prayer about holiness.

We learn in the Torah that we are supposed to be holy because God is holy (*Lev.* 19.2) and that the Jewish People is supposed to be a holy nation (*Ex.* 19.6). The Zohar makes it even clearer when it teaches, "We fill the earth with holiness through doing מִצְוֹת." How can doing מִצְוֹת fill the world with holiness?

Question ■ **: How can doing מִצְוֹת fill the world with holiness?** *Here are a number of different answers:* "מִצְוֹת point us to doing things that are holy." "מִצְוֹת make God happy, and God comes closer to us." "מִצְוֹת point our hearts toward seeing God's holiness." "מִצְוֹת inspire other people to do מִצְוֹת—and pretty soon the world is filled with people doing good things for each other."

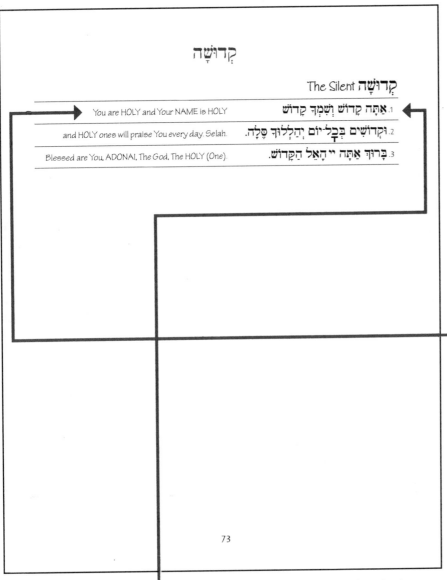

קְדוּשָׁה

The Silent קְדוּשָׁה

You are HOLY and Your NAME is HOLY	1. אַתָּה קָדוֹשׁ וְשִׁמְךָ קָדוֹשׁ
and HOLY ones will praise You every day. Selah.	2. וּקְדוֹשִׁים בְּכָל־יוֹם יְהַלְלוּךָ סֶּלָה.
Blessed are You, ADONAI, The God, The HOLY (One).	3. בָּרוּךְ אַתָּה יי הָאֵל הַקָּדוֹשׁ.

73

2. Practicing the Hebrew Text [a] INVITE students to work with a partner and practice the prayer. [b] READ or SING the prayers together as a class. [c] INVITE individual students or teams of students to perform individual lines or sections.

This page combines work on the root קדשׁ with practice of key phrases from the liturgy. We have had this root before.

HEBREW/ENGLISH TEXT

These two pages present the full text of the morning קְדוּשָׁה, both the silent and the oral version. They will be your core resource for drilling and mastering the performance of this prayer. They will also allow you to study the English translation and get an overview of the prayer.

 Big Ideas

1. When we enable students to perfect performances of the core liturgy we make it possible for them to far more easily participate in communal worship.

- The קְדוּשָׁה is one of the "high point" performance moments in the service. It makes the siddur top ten list.

- From God's holiness we gain the possibility to be holy.

 Learning Activities

1. Scanning the English text
2. Practicing the Hebrew text

You Know You've Succeeded When...

1. Students describe insights gained from looking at the English text.
2. Students practice their performance of the Hebrew text.

1. Scanning the English Text ▪ The silent קְדוּשָׁה is the first three lines of text on page 64. The first sentence teaches three things about God. Have your students list them:

a. God is holy.

b. God's name is holy

c. We get holy by praising God.

Ask students to explain the difference between these three things. (This is not easy.) One set of answers goes something like this.

a. **God is holy.** The Entity, God, is inherently holy.

b. **God's name is holy.** Our knowledge of God, our awareness of God, has the possibility of making us holy. God has lots of names. Each name tries to capture one aspect of God's totality (one attribute). So we call God "אֱמֶת" (Truth) because what God teaches is true. We call God "הַמָּקוֹם" (The Place) because God is everyplace. We call God "הָרַחֲמָן" (The Merciful One) because God is a source of mercy. Each of God's names helps us to become holy.

c. **And holiness comes in praising You every day.** The act of acknowledging God's holiness helps to make us holy. When we thank God for being holy—we come to adopt the same holiness in us.

NEW ROOT

On this page the root קדש is introduced.

Big Ideas

1. Mastering Hebrew roots dramatically improves comprehension.
2. Looking at words built out of a single root enhances an understanding of Hebrew thinking.
3. קדש is a foundational element in every Jew's basic vocabulary.
4. Recognizing קדש in context helps students to find a sense of meaning in many Hebrew prayers.

Learning Activities

1. Analysis of the root קדש
2. Identifying words built out of קדש
3. Reading and identifying activity

You Know You've Succeeded When...

1. Students can identify words with the קדש root.

1. Analysis of the Root ברא

a. Use the board or flashcards to introduce the root קדש and the words built out of it.

b. Establish the connection between the three words: קִדְּשָׁנוּ, מְקַדֵּשׁ, קָדוֹשׁ.

2. Identifying Words Built out of קדש

a. ASK: What word idea connects קִדְּשָׁנוּ, מְקַדֵּשׁ, קָדוֹשׁ?

b. ESTABLISH that "sacred" or "holy" is the core idea.

3. Reading and Identifying Activity

a. Let students prepare these lines with a Hevruta partner.

b. Go over the passage. Invite individual students to read. Ask the entire class to read out together the words built out of the root קדש.

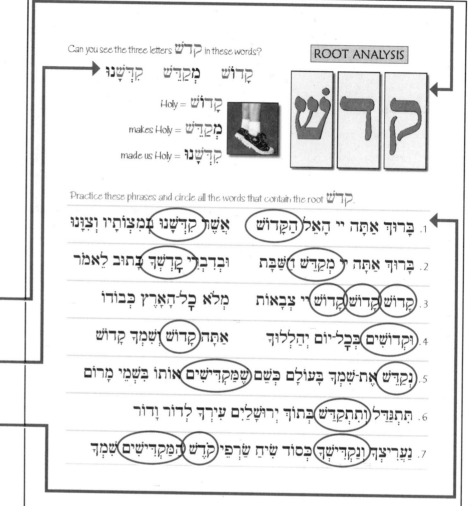

ROOT ANALYSIS

Can you see the three letters קדש in these words?

קָדוֹשׁ   מְקַדֵּשׁ   קִדְּשָׁנוּ

Holy = קָדוֹשׁ

makes Holy = מְקַדֵּשׁ

made us Holy = קִדְּשָׁנוּ

Practice these phrases and circle all the words that contain the root קדש.

1. בָּרוּךְ אַתָּה יי הָאֵל הַקָּדוֹשׁ   אֲשֶׁר קִדְּשָׁנוּ בְּמִצְוֹתָיו וְצִוָּנוּ

2. בָּרוּךְ אַתָּה יי מְקַדֵּשׁ הַשַּׁבָּת   וּבְדִבְרֵי קָדְשְׁךָ כָּתוּב לֵאמֹר

3. קָדוֹשׁ קָדוֹשׁ קָדוֹשׁ יי צְבָאוֹת   מְלֹא כָל־הָאָרֶץ כְּבוֹדוֹ

4. וּקְדוֹשִׁים בְּכָל־יוֹם יְהַלְלוּךָ   אַתָּה קָדוֹשׁ וְשִׁמְךָ קָדוֹשׁ

5. נְקַדֵּשׁ אֶת־שִׁמְךָ בָּעוֹלָם כְּשֵׁם שֶׁמַּקְדִּישִׁים אוֹתוֹ בִּשְׁמֵי מָרוֹם

6. תִּתְגַּדַּל וְתִתְקַדַּשׁ בְּתוֹךְ יְרוּשָׁלַיִם עִירְךָ לְדוֹר וָדוֹר

7. נַעֲרִיצְךָ וְנַקְדִּישְׁךָ כְּסוֹד שִׂיחַ שַׂרְפֵי קֹדֶשׁ הַמַּקְדִּישִׁים שְׁמֶךָ

74

74

TRANSLATION

Review the vocabulary and make your best guess at the meaning of the silent קְדוּשָׁה.

יוֹם

day

הלל

praise

קדש

holy

Take your best guess at the meaning of this text. Your teacher will help you with your translation.

אַתָּה קָדוֹשׁ וְשִׁמְךָ קָדוֹשׁ
וּקְדוֹשִׁים בְּכָל־יוֹם יְהַלְלוּךָ סֶּלָה.
בָּרוּךְ אַתָּה יי הָאֵל הַקָּדוֹשׁ.

You are holy and Your name is holy.

And holy every day praising You. Selah.

Praised are You Adonai, the God Holy.

---

word parts		words
in = בְּ	and = וְ	God = אֵל	name = שֵׁם
the = הַ	your = ךָ		all = כָּל

75

TRANSLATION/COMMENTARY

This page has students work on a translation of the silent קְדוּשָׁה.

Big Ideas

1. Growing and reinforcing Hebrew vocabulary leads to a growing affinity with the liturgy.
2. Applying the Hebrew they have to form rough translations of Hebrew prayers (a) helps students to feel closer to those texts, (b) reinforces the Hebrew they are learning and (c) develops a process they can continue to apply to the Siddur.

Learning Activities

1. Introducing/reviewing vocabulary
2. Working out a trial translation
3. Correcting translations
4. Prayer drill

You Know You've Succeeded When...

1. Students work out a reasonable translation of this text.
2. Students correct their translation.

1. Introducing/Reviewing Vocabulary ■ [a] Using VOCABULARY POSTERS and FLASHCARDS, introduce and drill the core vocabulary needed for this translation. [b] Some game playing or team competition is the perfect way to reinforce this vocabulary.

2. Working out a Trial Translation ■ [a] Working in pairs, students should develop their own best TRANSLATION. [b] They should not worry about being perfect—they should worry about coming close. EXPECT a working translation something like:

> **You are holy and Your name is holy.**
>
> **And holy every day praising You. Selah.**
>
> **Praised are You Adonai, the God Holy.**

3. Correcting Translations ■

(a) קְדוֹשִׁים בְּכָל־יוֹם יְהַלְלוּךָ סֶלָה is hard. It more or less means "Holiness comes through praising You every day."

(b) The word "סֶלָה" can't be translated. It more or less means "Yah."

(c) The phrase הָאֵל הַקָּדוֹשׁ means "the holy God."

4. Prayer Drill ■ Practice performing this portion of the prayer. SING or READ it together.

STORY

This page presents a midrashic origin for the קְדוּשָׁה as found in the story of Jacob's ladder.

Big Ideas

1. God is called הַמָקוֹם, The Place, because God is in every place.
2. People's actions can make God holy (or more holy, or more apparently holy).
3. The story of Jacob's ladder can give us powerful images to inspire our prayers.

Learning Activities

1. Read the story
2. Go over the story in Hevruta
3. Discuss the questions

You Know You've Succeeded When...

1. Students can retell the story.
2. Students can provide reasonable answers to the questions.

1. Read the Story ■ Either read aloud or have students read this story. The actual text here is pretty important. Then move to the discussion questions.

2. Go over the Story in Hevruta ■

3. Discuss the Questions ■

1. **Why is הַמָקוֹם (The Place) a name for God?** *Some good answers might be* (a) because God is in every place, (b) because God is our "place" (our connections), (c) because God is the place where our prayers go, etc.

2. **If God is holy to start with, how can our "righteous actions" make God holy?** *Students may come up with lots of good answers. But here is the core answer that we want to evolve. We cannot make God more holy in the absolute, but we can make God more holy in people's lives. We can let people know about, experience, feel, etc., God's holiness. And our holy actions can lead other people to more holy things, and they can lead others—and holiness can grow in the world.*

3. **How can knowing this story help you to know where to point your heart when you say the** קְדוּשָׁה**?** *Here are some great answers you may hear or you can add in:* (a) We can think of our prayers going up a ladder. (b) We can think of our good and holy deeds carrying our prayers to God. (c) We can imagine being Jacob dreaming of a connection to heaven. (d) We can think of the angels singing with us, etc.

Jacob Visits the Place

מָקוֹם is the Hebrew word for place. הַמָקוֹם, "The Place," is also a name for God.

Jacob left home, came to a place, and made camp. Using a rock for a pillow, he went to sleep and dreamed. In this מָקוֹם he met הַמָקוֹם. The midrash teaches, "Why is God called 'The Place'? Because in every place where there are righteous people God is there." Jacob learned that every מָקוֹם can be a place to discover הַמָקוֹם.

In his dream Jacob saw a ladder. Its feet were on the ground. Its head was in heaven. Angels were going up and down on the ladder. At the very top of the ladder Jacob saw "The Gates of Compassion" just below God's throne. When he awoke Jacob said, "This place is the Gate of Heaven. This is the place where the gates of heaven open to hear prayers. Here will be בֵּית אֵל, the House of God." Then Jacob said, "God is made holy through righteousness."

The angels answered and sang "בָּרוּךְ אַתָּה יי הָאֵל הַקָּדוֹשׁ." This was the first time the words that end the קְדוּשָׁה were used (*Gen. 28.10-22; P.R.E. 35*).

Questions

1. Why is הַמָקוֹם (The Place) a name for God?
2. If God is holy to start with, how can our "righteous actions" make God holy?
3. How can knowing this story help you to know where to point your heart when you say the קְדוּשָׁה?

76

קְדוּשַׁת הַיּוֹם

Lesson 20

Blank Page

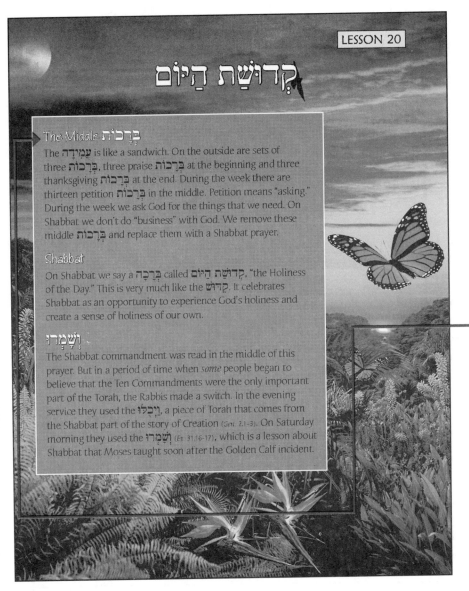

קְדוּשַׁת הַיוֹם

The Middle בְּרָכוֹת

The עֲמִידָה is like a sandwich. On the outside are sets of three בְּרָכוֹת, three praise בְּרָכוֹת at the beginning and three thanksgiving בְּרָכוֹת at the end. During the week there are thirteen petition בְּרָכוֹת in the middle. Petition means "asking." During the week we ask God for the things that we need. On Shabbat we don't do "business" with God. We remove these middle בְּרָכוֹת and replace them with a Shabbat prayer.

Shabbat

On Shabbat we say a בְּרָכָה called קְדוּשַׁת הַיוֹם, "the Holiness of the Day." This is very much like the קִדּוּשׁ. It celebrates Shabbat as an opportunity to experience God's holiness and create a sense of holiness of our own.

וְשָׁמְרוּ

The Shabbat commandment was read in the middle of this prayer. But in a period of time when *some* people began to believe that the Ten Commandments were the only important part of the Torah, the Rabbis made a switch. In the evening service they used the וַיְכֻלּוּ, a piece of Torah that comes from the Shabbat part of the story of Creation (Gen. 2.1-3). On Saturday morning they used the וְשָׁמְרוּ (Ex. 31.16-17), which is a lesson about Shabbat that Moses taught soon after the Golden Calf incident.

LESSON 20: INTRODUCTION

This page introduces the middle בְּרָכוֹת, קְדוּשַׁת הַיוֹם and שַׁבָּת.

Big Ideas

- The עֲמִידָה is like a sandwich: praise, petition, thanksgiving. We take out "petition" on Shabbat.
- קְדוּשַׁת הַיוֹם is the prayer that replaces the petition בְּרָכוֹת on Shabbat.
- One piece of Torah, וַיְכֻלּוּ, that talks about creation is used on Friday night. Another piece of Torah, וְשָׁמְרוּ, that connects to the Golden Calf is used on Saturday.

Learning Activities

1. Introducing the unit
2. Exploring the themes
3. Reviewing the key themes

You Know You've Succeeded When...

1. Students can describe the taking of the Torah out of the ark.
2. Students can state the two images that are used.

1. Introducing the Unit ■

2. Exploring the Themes ■ CONVEY THE INFORMATION IN THE INTRODUCTION: Do one of the following. [a] DESCRIBE the information to your students. [b] READ out loud and DISCUSS this information. [c] ASSIGN your students to READ the information on their own and then DISCUSS it.

3. Reviewing the Key Themes ■

Redemption: One of the tasks you will need to do here is to define "redemption." Literally, to "redeem" something is to "restore" it. When we were slaves in Egypt, God "redeemed" us and brought us to freedom. In general usage, redeem means to save or to rescue. The final redemption is when God (with our help) perfects and heals the world.

The Middle בְּרָכוֹת: (a) The עֲמִידָה is usually 3 praise בְּרָכוֹת, 13 petition בְּרָכוֹת and 3 petition בְּרָכוֹת; (b) On Shabbat we don't say the petition prayers because that is too much like work.

Shabbat: (a) A prayer called קְדוּשַׁת הַיוֹם replaces the petitions on Shabbat; (b) Shabbat has two big themes: Creation and the Exodus. (We learned this in the קִדּוּשׁ.) This is now extended into קְדוּשַׁת הַיוֹם in the עֲמִידָה.

(a) וַיְכֻלּוּ (Genesis 2.1-3) is used on Friday night and connects us to creation; (b) וְשָׁמְרוּ (Ex. 31.16-17) is used on Saturday morning (and before lunch) and connects to Egypt and the Exodus

TRANSLATION AND TEXT

This page contains the Hebrew and English text of the קְדוּשַׁת הַיּוֹם שֶׁל שַׁבָּת. It should be used for both introducing the prayer and practicing and perfecting its performance.

Big Ideas

1. When we enable students to perfect performances of the core liturgy we make it possible for them to far more easily participate in communal worship.
2. By scanning the English of prayers students can grow insights into the meaning of the liturgy.
3. Perfecting a performance of the וַיְכֻלּוּ will make both the Shabbat עֲמִידָה and the Saturday morning קִדּוּשׁ possible.
4. People rest on Shabbat because God rested.

Learning Activities

1. Scanning the English text
2. Practicing the Hebrew text

You Know You've Succeeded When...

1. Students describe insights gained from looking at the English text.
2. Students practice their performance of the Hebrew text.

1. Scanning the English Text ■ INVITE students to SCAN the English translation

of these prayers. ASK them what "big ideas" they can find by looking. Look at the differences in the liturgical formulae.

Lines 1-9

Ask: What things does this biblical text teach us about Shabbat?

Answers: (a) Israel is commanded to "keep" it. (b) It is a "sign" of the covenant between God and Israel. (c) We rest because God rested.

Lines 10-20

Ask: Have your students list the things that we ask for in this prayer.

Answer: (a) enjoy our REST (b) Make us Holy through Your MITZVOT (c) give us a piece of Your TORAH (d) NOURISH us with Your goodness (e) MAKE-US-HAPPY through Your REDEMPTION (d) PURIFY our hearts to Your WORK (e) give-us-as-an-INHERITANCE Your HOLY SHABBAT (f) May Israel REST on it MAKING Your NAME holy.

Ask: How does resting on Shabbat get us to the rest of the things on the list?

Answer: It is through resting on Shabbat that we get a chance to do the "spiritual work" to make the other connections.

2. Practicing the Hebrew Text ■ [a] INVITE students to work with a partner and

practice the prayer. [b] READ or SING the prayers together as a class. [c] INVITE individual students or teams of students to perform individual lines or sections.

קְדוּשַׁת הַיּוֹם

And the heavens and the earth	1. וַיְכֻלּוּ הַשָּׁמַיִם וְהָאָרֶץ
all their accessories were FINISHED.	2. וְכָל־צְבָאָם.
God FINISHED on the Seventh Day	3. וַיְכַל אֱלֹהִים בַּיּוֹם הַשְּׁבִיעִי
the work that was done,	4. מְלַאכְתּוֹ אֲשֶׁר עָשָׂה
God made a SABBATH on the Seventh Day	5. וַיִּשְׁבֹּת בַּיּוֹם הַשְּׁבִיעִי
from all the work that was done.	6. מִכָּל־מְלַאכְתּוֹ אֲשֶׁר עָשָׂה.
God BLESSED the Seventh Day	7. וַיְבָרֶךְ אֱלֹהִים אֶת־יוֹם הַשְּׁבִיעִי
and made it HOLY	8. וַיְקַדֵּשׁ אֹתוֹ
because on it God RESTED from all the work	9. כִּי בוֹ שָׁבַת מִכָּל־מְלַאכְתּוֹ
that God did during CREATION.	10. אֲשֶׁר בָּרָא אֱלֹהִים לַעֲשׂוֹת.
Our God and God of our Ancestors,	11. אֱלֹהֵינוּ וֵאלֹהֵי אֲבוֹתֵינוּ
enjoy our REST.	12. רְצֵה בִמְנוּחָתֵנוּ.
Make us Holy through Your MITZVOT	13. קַדְּשֵׁנוּ בְּמִצְוֹתֶיךָ
and give us a piece of Your TORAH,	14. וְתֵן חֶלְקֵנוּ בְּתוֹרָתֶךָ
NOURISH us with Your goodness	15. שַׂבְּעֵנוּ מִטּוּבֶךָ
And MAKE-US-HAPPY through Your REDEMPTION,	16. וְשַׂמְּחֵנוּ בִּישׁוּעָתֶךָ
PURIFY our hearts to Your WORK in truth.	17. וְטַהֵר לִבֵּנוּ לְעָבְדְּךָ בֶּאֱמֶת.
ADONAI our God, give-us-as-an-INHERITANCE	18. וְהַנְחִילֵנוּ יי אֱלֹהֵינוּ
in LOVE and because You WANT Your HOLY SHABBAT.	19. בְּאַהֲבָה וּבְרָצוֹן שַׁבַּת קָדְשֶׁךָ.
May Israel REST on it MAKING Your NAME holy.	20. וְיָנוּחוּ בָהּ יִשְׂרָאֵל מְקַדְּשֵׁי שְׁמֶךָ.
Blessed be You, ADONAI, the One-Who-makes SHABBAT HOLY.	21. בָּרוּךְ אַתָּה יי מְקַדֵּשׁ הַשַּׁבָּת.

78

Review the vocabulary and make your best guess at the meaning of this phrase from וַיְכֻלּוּ

קרֹשׁ	שְׁבִיעִי	יוֹם	בָּרוּךְ
holy	seven	day	bless

Take your best guess at the meaning of this text. Your teacher will help you with your translation.

וַיְבָרֶךְ אֱלֹהִים אֶת־יוֹם הַשְּׁבִיעִי וַיְקַדֵּשׁ אֹתוֹ

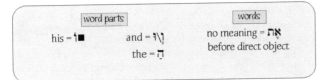

And God blessed the Seventh day and made it holy.

_____

_____

word parts		words
his = וֹ ■	and = וַ\	no meaning = אֶת
	the = הַ	before direct object

TRANSLATION

This page concludes this lesson by allowing students to (a) work out a translation of the first half of וַיְכֻלּוּ and (b) talk about the phrase "making Shabbat."

Big Ideas

1. Growing and reinforcing Hebrew vocabulary leads to a growing affinity with the liturgy.
2. Applying the Hebrew they have to form rough translations of Hebrew prayers (a) helps students to feel closer to those texts, (b) reinforces the Hebrew they are learning. (c) develops a process they can continue to apply to the Siddur.

Learning Activities

1. Introducing/reviewing vocabulary
2. Working out a trial translation
3. Correcting translations
4. Prayer drill

You Know You've Succeeded When...

1. Students work out a reasonable translation of this text.
2. Students correct their translation.

1. **Introducing/Reviewing Vocabulary** ■ [a] Using VOCABULARY POSTERS and FLASHCARDS, introduce and drill the core vocabulary needed for this translation. [b] Some game playing or team competition is the perfect way to reinforce this vocabulary.

2. **Working out a Trial Translation** ■ [a] Working in pairs, students should develop their own best TRANSLATION. [b] They should not worry about being perfect—they should worry about coming close. EXPECT a working translation something like: **And bless God the Seventh day and holy it.**

3. **Correcting Translations** ■ To help them fix this you will want to help with word order, e.g., "And God blessed the Seventh Day and made it Holy."

4. **Prayer Drill** ■ Practice performing this portion of the prayer. SING or READ it together.

STORY: THE SABBATH SPICE

This classic story highlights the specialness of Shabbat.

Big Idea
- Shabbat is a special time.

Learning Activities
1. Read the story
2. Go over the story in Hevruta
3. Discuss the questions

You Know You've Succeeded When...
1. Students can retell the story.
2. Students can provide reasonable answers to the questions.

1. Read the Story ■ Either read aloud or have students read this story. The actual text here is pretty important. Then move to the discussion questions.

2. Go over the Story in Hevruta ■

3. Discuss the Questions ■
1. **What was in the cold meal that made it so special?** It was filled with the holiness of Shabbat—the spice of Shabbat.
2. **How can knowing this story help us to know where to point our hearts when we say the קְדוּשַׁת הַיּוֹם?** Help students focus on ways to make Shabbat special and holy.

The Emperor, the Rabbi and a Spice Called Shabbat

Antoninus was a Roman Emperor. He had a good friend named Rabbi Yehudah ha-Nasi. One Shabbat, Rabbi Yehudah prepared lunch for his friend. The food was cold because the Rabbi did not cook on Shabbat. Still, Antoninus pronounced everything "delicious."

"Mmmmm," said Rabbi Yehudah, raising his eyebrows like he knew a secret but couldn't tell.

Later that week the Emperor again went to the rabbi's house for dinner. This time the rabbi served him a piping hot meal. Antoninus tasted everything.

"The meat is okay," he said to the rabbi, "and the vegetables aren't bad, but I enjoyed the last meal much more. This food is missing something."

Rabbi Yehudah loved his friend and so he tried not to laugh.

"Well, something is missing," said the Emperor. "Did you forget something, or is it a secret recipe that has been handed down from one Jewish family to another year after year after year? Come on, you can tell me. What is it?"

"Okay, my friend, you're right," replied Rabbi Yehudah. "Something is missing. But you won't find it in the pantry. You won't find it in the cellar either. You won't find it in the cabinet, in the rear or on top. You won't even find it in my box of "secret recipes that have been handed down from one Jewish family to another for years after year after year."

Rabbi Yehudah continued, "What's missing is a spice that can't be grown, can't be mixed, can't be found or tasted anywhere. You see," he said, "what's really missing is not an ingredient at all, but the Shabbat itself." (Talmud Shabbat 119a)

Questions
1. What was in the cold meal on Shabbat that made it so special?
2. How can knowing this story help us to know where to point our hearts when we say the קְדוּשַׁת הַיּוֹם?

80

בִּרְכוֹת שָׁלוֹם

This unit introduces שִׂים שָׁלוֹם.

Lesson 21

Lesson 22

Blank Page

בִּרְכַּת שָׁלוֹם is:

- the last of three thanksgiving בְּרָכוֹת that end the עֲמִידָה and the very last בְּרָכָה in the עֲמִידָה.

- a בְּרָכָה that asks for both world peace and personal inner peace.

- a prayer that has two versions. In Ashkenazic traditions, שִׂים שָׁלוֹם is said at morning services. שָׁלוֹם רָב is said at afternoon, מוּסָף and evening services. Sefardim do it differently.

At the end of the service in the Temple the כֹּהֲנִים (priests) would bless the people. This was their way of performing a biblical מִצְוָה, "The כֹּהֲנִים should put My Name on the People of Israel—and I will bless them" (Num. 6.27). שָׁלוֹם is one of God's names.

When the Temple was destroyed and the עֲמִידָה replaced the sacrifices, בִּרְכַּת שָׁלוֹם became its final בְּרָכָה. בִּרְכַּת שָׁלוֹם became the day-to-day replacement for בִּרְכַּת־כֹּהֲנִים in the Temple. This pattern followed a lesson taught by Rabbi Eleazar ha-Kappar, "Great is peace. It is the end of all בְּרָכוֹת" (Sifrei, Numbers, 42).

FOOTNOTE: Ashkenazic Jews are those who came from Christian countries in Northern and Eastern Europe. Sefardic Jews are those who come from Moslem countries in Spain, Northern Africa, and the Middle East. Some Sefardic Jews moved to Holland, Rome, and Rhodes.

LESSON 21

LESSON 21: INTRODUCTION

This page introduces שִׂים שָׁלוֹם as "the end of all blessings."

Big Ideas

1. בִּרְכַּת שָׁלוֹם has two versions in many traditions and is the last בְּרָכָה in the עֲמִידָה.

2. It comes from the "priestly blessings."

3. It is called the "end" of all בְּרָכוֹת.

Learning Activities

1. Introducing the unit
2. Exploring the themes
3. Reviewing the key themes

You Know You've Succeeded When...

1. Students can explain the structure, form, location, theme and sources for בִּרְכַּת שָׁלוֹם.

2. Students can explain why בִּרְכַּת שָׁלוֹם is the final בְּרָכָה in the עֲמִידָה.

1. Introducing the Unit ■

2. Exploring the Themes ■ CONVEY THE INFORMATION IN THE INTRODUCTION: Do one of the following. [a] DESCRIBE the information to your students. [b] READ out loud and DISCUSS this information. [c] ASSIGN your students to READ the information on their own and then DISCUSS it.

3. Reviewing the Key Themes ■

- This is the last בְּרָכָה in the עֲמִידָה.
- It is about both world peace and inner peace.
- In Ashkenazic tradition שִׂים שָׁלוֹם is said in the morning and שָׁלוֹם רָב is said in the afternoon and evening.
- This בְּרָכָה evolves from the priestly benediction.
- שָׁלוֹם is the "end of all blessings."

The Question: Why should שָׁלוֹם be "the end" of all בְּרָכוֹת?

There are two answers.

a. The literal answer: It is the last בְּרָכָה in the עֲמִידָה. The end!

b. The spiritual answer: It is the final step. It is the end goal of both society and individuals. All of our hard work on us and on the world is aimed to שָׁלוֹם. That makes it the end, the final request.

TRANSLATION AND TEXT

We have the Hebrew drill text and an English translation to help students get an overview of שִׂים שָׁלוֹם. Later in the unit we will look at שָׁלוֹם רָב. The commentary provides two answers to the question on the previous page.

Big Ideas

1. When we enable students to perfect performances of the core liturgy we make it possible for them to far more easily participate in communal worship.
2. By scanning the English of prayers students can grow insights into the meaning of the liturgy.
3. Mastering a performance of שִׂים שָׁלוֹם will facilitate praying it.
4. Looking at the translation helps students get a feel for the prayer.

Learning Activities

1. Scanning the English text
2. Practicing the Hebrew text

You Know You've Succeeded When...

1. Students describe insights gained from looking at the English text.
2. Students practice their performance of the Hebrew text.

1. Scanning the English Text ■ INVITE students to SCAN the English translation of these prayers. ASK them what "big ideas" they can find by looking. Look at the differences in the liturgical formulae.

1. Ask students why the image of God's face is used in this prayer. The answer will be found below. It is an image that comes from the priestly benediction in the Torah.
2. Ask students to pick one image from this prayer that they really like. Have them explain and share their images.

2. Practicing the Hebrew Text ■ [a] INVITE students to work with a partner and practice the prayer. [b] READ or SING the prayers together as a class. [c] INVITE individual students or teams of students to perform individual lines or sections.

שָׁלוֹם רָב

Much PEACE	1. שָׁלוֹם רָב
on Israel, Your People, put forever	2. עַל יִשְׂרָאֵל עַמְּךָ תָּשִׂים לְעוֹלָם,
Because You are the ONE, the RULER	3. כִּי אַתָּה הוּא מֶלֶךְ
The Master of all PEACE.	4. אָדוֹן לְכָל־הַשָּׁלוֹם.
And (may it be) good in YOUR EYES	5. וְטוֹב בְּעֵינֶיךָ
to bless Your people Israel	6. לְבָרֵךְ אֶת עַמְּךָ יִשְׂרָאֵל
in all times, in all hours, with Your PEACE.	7. בְּכָל־עֵת וּבְכָל־שָׁעָה בִּשְׁלוֹמֶךָ.
Praised be You, ADONAI	8. בָּרוּךְ אַתָּה יי
The ONE-Who-BLESSES God's people Israel	9. הַמְבָרֵךְ אֶת־עַמּוֹ יִשְׂרָאֵל
with PEACE.	10. בַּשָּׁלוֹם.

82

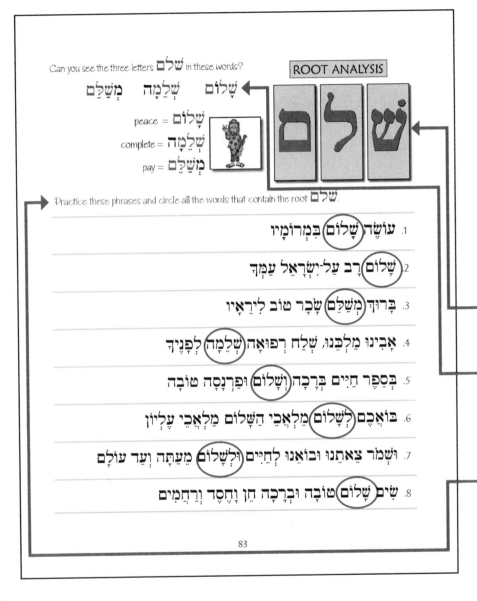

Can you see the three letters שלם in these words?

מְשַׁלֵם   שְׁלֵמָה   שָׁלוֹם

ROOT ANALYSIS

peace = שָׁלוֹם

complete = שְׁלֵמָה

pay = מְשַׁלֵם

Practice these phrases and circle all the words that contain the root שלם.

1. עוֹשֶׂה שָׁלוֹם בִּמְרוֹמָיו

2. שָׁלוֹם רָב עַל־יִשְׂרָאֵל עַמְּךָ

3. בָּרוּךְ מְשַׁלֵם שָׂכָר טוֹב לִירֵאָיו

4. אָבִינוּ מַלְכֵּנוּ, שְׁלַח רְפוּאָה שְׁלֵמָה לְפָנֶיךָ

5. בְּסֵפֶר חַיִּים בְּרָכָה וְשָׁלוֹם וּפַרְנָסָה טוֹבָה

6. בּוֹאֲכֶם לְשָׁלוֹם מַלְאֲכֵי הַשָּׁלוֹם מַלְאֲכֵי עֶלְיוֹן

7. וּשְׁמֹר צֵאתֵנוּ וּבוֹאֵנוּ לְחַיִּים וּלְשָׁלוֹם מֵעַתָּה וְעַד עוֹלָם

8. שִׂים שָׁלוֹם טוֹבָה וּבְרָכָה חֵן וָחֶסֶד רַחֲמִים

83

ROOT ANALYSIS

This page works on the root שלם, the theme word of these prayers.

Big Ideas

1. Mastering Hebrew roots dramatically improves comprehension.
2. Looking at words built out of a single root enhances an understanding of Hebrew thinking.
3. The Hebrew word שָׁלוֹם really means "whole" or "complete." The English word "peace" means "quiet" or "still."
4. Perception of roots in context builds both comprehension and connection.

Learning Activities

1. Analysis of the root שלם
2. Identifying words built out of שלם
3. Reading and identifying activity

You Know You've Succeeded When...

- Students can identify words with the שלם root.

1. Analysis of the Root שלם ▪

a. Use the board or flashcards to introduce the root שלם and the words built out of it.

b. Establish the connection between the three words: שָׁלוֹם, שְׁלֵמָה, מְשַׁלֵם.

2. Identifying Words Built out of שלם ▪

a. ASK: What word idea connects שָׁלוֹם, שְׁלֵמָה, מְשַׁלֵם?

b. ESTABLISH that the שלם root really means "whole" or "complete." Have students connect the meanings of the three words. Here is the key: The Jewish vision of peace has to do with "wholeness." Likewise, when one pays a bill, one is completing a transaction.

3. Reading and Identifying Activity ▪

a. Let students prepare these lines with a Hevruta partner.

b. Go over the passage. Invite individual students to read. Ask the entire class to read out together the words built out of the root שלם.

TRANSLATION

On this page we work out a translation of the first line of שִׂים שָׁלוֹם and look at its six requests.

Big Ideas

1. Growing and reinforcing Hebrew vocabulary leads to a growing affinity with the liturgy.
2. Applying the Hebrew they have to form rough translations of Hebrew prayers (a) helps students to feel closer to those texts, (b) reinforces the Hebrew they are learning and (c) develops a process they can continue to apply to the Siddur.

Learning Activities

1. Introducing/reviewing vocabulary
2. Working out a trial translation
3. Correcting translations
4. Prayer drill

You Know You've Succeeded When...

1. Students work out a reasonable translation of this text.
2. Students correct their translation.

1. Introducing/Reviewing Vocabulary ■ [a] Using VOCABULARY POSTERS and FLASHCARDS, introduce and drill the core vocabulary needed for this translation. [b] Some game playing or team competition is the perfect way to reinforce this vocabulary.

2. Working out a Trial Translation ■ [a] Working in pairs, students should develop their own best TRANSLATION. [b] They should not worry about being perfect—they should worry about coming close. EXPECT a working translation something like:
Put peace, good, blessing, favor, kindness
And mercy on us, and on call Israel your people

3. Correcting Translations ■

שִׂים should be understood as "give"

טוֹבָה = goodness

רַחֲמִים should be understood as "mercy."

עָלֵינוּ here is "for us" and וְעַל is "and for"

4. Prayer Drill ■ Practice performing this portion of the prayer. SING or READ it together.

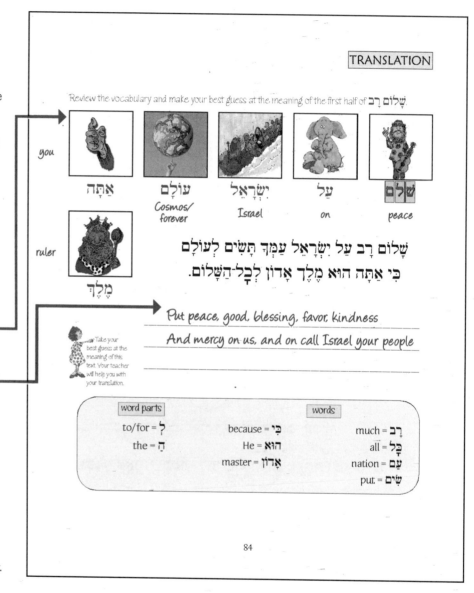

TRANSLATION

Review the vocabulary and make your best guess at the meaning of the first half of רַב שָׁלוֹם.

you אַתָּה	עוֹלָם Cosmos/forever	יִשְׂרָאֵל Israel	עַל on	שָׁלוֹם peace
ruler מֶלֶךְ				

שָׁלוֹם רַב עַל יִשְׂרָאֵל עַמְּךָ תָּשִׂים לְעוֹלָם
כִּי אַתָּה הוּא מֶלֶךְ אָדוֹן לְכָל־הַשָּׁלוֹם.

Take your best guess at the meaning of this text. Your teacher will help you with your translation.

Put peace, good, blessing, favor, kindness
And mercy on us, and on call Israel your people

word parts		words
to/for = לְ	because = כִּי	much = רַב
the = הַ	He = הוּא	all = כָּל
	master = אָדוֹן	nation = עַם
		put = שִׂים

84

TRANSLATION

Review the vocabulary and make your best guess at the meaning of the remainder of שָׁלוֹם רַב.

peace

Israel

bless

eyes

good

Take your best guess at the meaning of this text. Your teacher will help you with your translation.

וְטוֹב בְּעֵינֶיךָ לְבָרֵךְ אֶת־עַמְּךָ יִשְׂרָאֵל
בְּכָל־עֵת וּבְכָל־שָׁעָה בִּשְׁלוֹמֶךָ.
בָּרוּךְ אַתָּה יי הַמְבָרֵךְ אֶת־עַמּוֹ יִשְׂרָאֵל בַּשָּׁלוֹם.

And good in your eyes to bless your people Israel

In all time in all hour in your peace.

Blessed be You Adonai the bless of His People Israel in peace.

---

word parts		words	
your = ךָ	and = וְ/וּ	season = עֵת	nation = עַם
to/for = לְ	in/with = בְּ	time = שָׁעָה	all = כָּל

85

LESSON 22: TRANSLATION

This page looks at the "ending" of שִׂים שָׁלוֹם and works out a translation.

Big Ideas

1. Growing and reinforcing Hebrew vocabulary leads to a growing affinity with the liturgy.
2. Applying the Hebrew they have to form rough translations of Hebrew prayers (a) helps students to feel closer to those texts, (b) reinforces the Hebrew they are learning and (c) develops a process they can continue to apply to the Siddur.

Learning Activities

1. Introducing/reviewing vocabulary
2. Working out a trial translation
3. Correcting translations
4. Prayer drill

You Know You've Succeeded When...

1. Students work out a reasonable translation of this text.
2. Students correct their translation.

1. Introducing/Reviewing Vocabulary ■ [a] Using VOCABULARY POSTERS and FLASHCARDS, introduce and drill the core vocabulary needed for this translation. [b] Some game playing or team competition is the perfect way to reinforce this vocabulary.

2. Working out a Trial Translation ■ [a] Working in pairs, students should develop their own best TRANSLATION. [b] They should not worry about being perfect—they should worry about coming close. EXPECT a working translation something like:

And good in your eyes to bless your people Israel
In all time in all hour in your peace.
Blessed be You Adonai the bless of His People Israel in peace.

3. Correcting Translations ■

a. וְטוֹב בְּעֵינֶיךָ לְבָרֵךְ–and "MAY" it be good in your eyes.

b. וּבְכָל־שָׁעָה בְּכָל־עֵת–"AT" all times "AT EVERY" hour

c. הַמְבָרֵךְ–"The One-Who-blesses"

4. Prayer Drill ■ Practice performing this portion of the prayer. SING or READ it together.

STORY: JACOB AND ESAU MAKE PEACE

This page presents an origin story for בִּרְכוֹת שָׁלוֹם.

Big Ideas

• Jacob and Esau represent the perfect example not only of brothers who fight but also of brothers who make up.

• בִּרְכוֹת שָׁלוֹם are also about שָׁלוֹם בַּיִת, family peace.

Learning Activities

1. Read the story
2. Go over the story in Hevruta
3. Discuss the questions

You Know You've Succeeded When...

1. Students can retell the story.
2. Students can provide reasonable answers to the questions.

1. Read the Story ■ Either read aloud or have students read this story. The actual text here is pretty important. Then move to the discussion questions.

2. Go over the Story in Hevruta ■

3. Discuss the Questions ■

1. **What made Jacob ready to make peace? What made Esau ready to make peace?** *Both answers are specifically pointed to in the story:* (a) For Jacob, spending twenty years raising a family away from home made him ready to go home and make peace. (b) For Esau, seeing his brother weak and with family meant that he was no longer a threat. *Students might add,* "Enough time went by." "They both remembered that they were brothers." "Each got older and less childish."

2. **Explain the connection between inner peace and political peace in this story.** *Here is the idea we are going for:* Both Jacob and Esau were ready to make peace. They had gotten "inside" to a place where they could make a political peace between their two groups. *Students may get here by saying,* "Each of them changed." "Each felt something new." *Or by restating the basic facts,* "Jacob was homesick and Esau felt safe."

3. **How can knowing this story help you know where to point your heart when you say בִּרְכַּת שָׁלוֹם?** *Here are some answers you can expect.* "You have to be ready for peace." "You make peace first on the inside." "We can be like Jacob and Esau when we say this prayer and get past our fighting."

From before their birth, brothers Jacob and Esau struggled with each other. As unborn babies they wrestled in the womb. Jacob first tricked Esau out of his birthright and then later stole his father's blessing. Jacob ran away from home and went back to Padan Aram in "the old country" to keep his brother from killing him. He spent twenty years away from home, married two women and had twelve children. Before he headed back home he prayed to God, "Let me return to my father's home in peace" *(Gen. 28.21)*.

When Jacob and his holy family were about to meet Esau—and his army of four hundred was moving toward him—Jacob prepared three things: peace-offerings, a prayer, and to fight back. He spent the night alone and wound up wrestling with a stranger who for him was the spirit of his brother. He walked away crippled and with a new name, יִשְׂרָאֵל. When Esau came ready for war he saw a crippled man surrounded by women and children. He felt safe. He was transformed, too. Both brothers were now ready to make peace. At that moment the angels sang, "שָׁלוֹם רַב עַל יִשְׂרָאֵל תָּשִׂים לְעוֹלָם" *(Tanhuma, Yashan 6; Kallah Rabbati 3; Rashbam ad loc)*.

Questions

1. What made Jacob ready to make peace? What made Esau ready to make peace?
2. Explain the connection between inner peace and political peace in this story.
3. How can knowing this story help you know where to point your heart when you say בִּרְכַּת שָׁלוֹם?

86

עָלֵינוּ

This is a one-lesson unit on the עָלֵינוּ, that deals with the beginning of the עָלֵינוּ and focuses on the central theme of תִּקּוּן עוֹלָם.

Lesson 23

Page 87: We introduce the עָלֵינוּ in an historical context.

Pages 88: Then we look at the Hebrew text and translation of the complete עָלֵינוּ.

Page 89: We translate the beginning of the עָלֵינוּ

Page 89: We end with the story *The Jewel*, another statement of the theme of תִּקּוּן עוֹלָם.

Blank Page

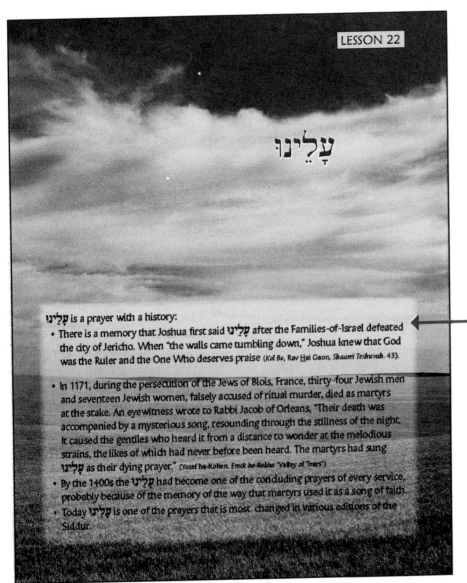

LESSON 22

עָלֵינוּ

עָלֵינוּ is a prayer with a history:

- There is a memory that Joshua first said עָלֵינוּ after the Families-of-Israel defeated the city of Jericho. When "the walls came tumbling down," Joshua knew that God was the Ruler and the One Who deserves praise (*Kol Bo, Rav Hai Gaon, Shaarei Teshuvah.* 43).

- In 1171, during the persecution of the Jews of Blois, France, thirty-four Jewish men and seventeen Jewish women, falsely accused of ritual murder, died as martyrs at the stake. An eyewitness wrote to Rabbi Jacob of Orleans, "Their death was accompanied by a mysterious song, resounding through the stillness of the night. It caused the gentiles who heard it from a distance to wonder at the melodious strains, the likes of which had never before been heard. The martyrs had sung עָלֵינוּ as their dying prayer." (*Yosef ha-Kohen, Emek ha-Bakha "Valley of Tears"*)

- By the 1400s the עָלֵינוּ had become one of the concluding prayers of every service, probably because of the memory of the way that martyrs used it as a song of faith.

- Today עָלֵינוּ is one of the prayers that is most changed in various editions of the Siddur.

LESSON 22: עָלֵינוּ INTRODUCTION

This introduction describes עָלֵינוּ.

Big Ideas

1. עָלֵינוּ is a prayer with a series of stories: (a) Joshua led the people in עָלֵינוּ after the walls came tumbling down, (b) Rav created it as part of the Rosh ha-Shanah מוּסָף service, (c) in 1711 the Jews of Blois sang it as they were martyred, (d) by 1400 it became part of every service, (e) Pesach Peter, an apostate, spread the lie that it was a slur to Christianity.
2. עָלֵינוּ is the "theological summary" at the end of a service.

Learning Activities

1. Introducing the unit
2. Exploring the themes
3. Reviewing the key themes

You Know You've Succeeded When...

1. Students can describe the history of עָלֵינוּ.
2. Students can identify the big ideas in עָלֵינוּ.

1. Using the Purple Box ■ USE the purple box to help students anticipate the things that will be covered in this unit.

2. Introducing the Unit ■

3. Exploring the Themes ■ CONVEY THE INFORMATION IN THE INTRODUCTION. Do one of the following. [a] DESCRIBE the information to your students. [b] READ aloud and DISCUSS this information. [c] ASSIGN your students to READ the information on their own and then DISCUSS it.

4. Reviewing the Key Themes ■

a. עָלֵינוּ has a history (review each story).

b. עָלֵינוּ is a "theological summary." Read and discuss the Joel Sirkes quotation.

TEXT AND TRANSLATION

This page contains the Hebrew and English text of the עָלֵינוּ blessing.

Big Ideas

1. When we enable students to perfect performances of core liturgy we make it possible for them to far more easily participate in communal worship.
2. By scanning the English of prayers students can grow insights into the meaning of the liturgy.
3. We have an obligation to praise God.
4. The world will be fixed (תִּקוּן עוֹלָם).
5. One day everyone will know God.

Learning Activities

1. Scanning the English text
2. Practicing the Hebrew text

You Know You've Succeeded When...

1. Students describe insights gained from looking at the English text.
2. Students practice their performance of the Hebrew text.

1. Scanning the English Text ■ INVITE students to SCAN the English translation of these prayers. ASK them what "big ideas" they can find by looking.

INSIGHTS that might be shared:

- We have an obligation to praise God.
- Jews have a unique role in history.
- תִּקוּן עוֹלָם will happen.
- God's name will be One.

2. Practicing the Hebrew Text ■ [a] INVITE students to work with a partner and practice the prayer. [b] READ or SING the prayers together as a class. [c] INVITE individual students or teams of students to perform individual lines or sections.

עָלֵינוּ

It is our job to praise the MASTER-of-All	1. עָלֵינוּ לְשַׁבֵּחַ לַאֲדוֹן הַכֹּל,
To grant GREATness	2. לָתֵת גְּדֻלָּה
to the ONE-Who-Stages CREATION,	3. לְיוֹצֵר בְּרֵאשִׁית,
The ONE-Who-Didn't-Make-Us	4. שֶׁלֹּא עָשָׂנוּ
like the other NATIONS-of-the-LANDS	5. כְּגוֹיֵי הָאֲרָצוֹת
and didn't PUT our fate	6. וְלֹא שָׂמָנוּ
with the other FAMILIES-of-the-EARTH	7. כְּמִשְׁפְּחוֹת הָאֲדָמָה,
and did not PUT our PORTION with theirs.	8. שֶׁלֹּא שָׂם חֶלְקֵנוּ כָּהֶם
and our LOT with the MANY.	9. וְגוֹרָלֵנוּ כְּכָל-הֲמוֹנָם.
The One Who GAVE us the Torah of truth	שֶׁנָּתַן לָנוּ תּוֹרַת אֱמֶת
and planted eternal life within us.	וְחַיֵּי עוֹלָם נָטַע בְּתוֹכֵנוּ.
We BOW & BEND & FLATTEN-in-THANKS	10. וַאֲנַחְנוּ כּוֹרְעִים וּמִשְׁתַּחֲוִים וּמוֹדִים
Before the RULER-of-RULERS	11. לִפְנֵי מֶלֶךְ מַלְכֵי הַמְּלָכִים
The HOLY ONE-Who-is-to-be-BLESSED.	12. הַקָּדוֹשׁ בָּרוּךְ הוּא.
The ONE-WHO-Spread-out the HEAVENS	13. שֶׁהוּא נוֹטֶה שָׁמַיִם
and laid the earth's foundations	14. וְיוֹסֵד אָרֶץ,
and has the SEAT-of-Homage in the heavens above	15. וּמוֹשַׁב יְקָרוֹ בַּשָּׁמַיִם מִמַּעַל
and God's NEIGHBORHOOD-of-Power in the highest heights.	16. וּשְׁכִינַת עֻזּוֹ בְּגָבְהֵי מְרוֹמִים.
God is our God—there is none other.	17. הוּא אֱלֹהֵינוּ, אֵין עוֹד.
In TRUTH God is RULER—NOTHING compares	18. אֱמֶת מַלְכֵּנוּ, אֶפֶס זוּלָתוֹ,
as it is WRITTEN:	19. כַּכָּתוּב בְּתוֹרָתוֹ:
"And You are to KNOW today in the thoughts of your HEART,	20. וְיָדַעְתָּ הַיּוֹם וַהֲשֵׁבֹתָ אֶל לְבָבֶךָ,
that ADONAI is the ONE God	21. כִּי יי הוּא הָאֱלֹהִים
both in HEAVEN ABOVE and on EARTH below—	22. בַּשָּׁמַיִם מִמַּעַל וְעַל הָאָרֶץ מִתָּחַת,
NONE can COMPARE" (Deuteronomy 4.39).	23. אֵין עוֹד.

88

BECAUSE of this, we WISH from You	24. עַל כֵּן נְקַוֶּה לְּךָ
ADONAI, our God,	25. יְיָ אֱלֹהֵינוּ
To soon SEE the WONDER of your strength	26. לִרְאוֹת מְהֵרָה בְּתִפְאֶרֶת עֻזֶּךָ,
to terminate idolatry from the earth	27. לְהַעֲבִיר גִּלּוּלִים מִן הָאָרֶץ
and completely cut off the false gods—	28. וְהָאֱלִילִים כָּרוֹת יִכָּרֵתוּן,
to do TIKKUN OLAM in God's EMPIRE	29. לְתַקֵּן עוֹלָם בְּמַלְכוּת שַׁדַּי
and all humanity will CALL Your NAME	30. וְכָל־בְּנֵי בָשָׂר יִקְרְאוּ בִשְׁמֶךָ,
to RETURN to You all the WICKED-of-the-EARTH.	31. לְהַפְנוֹת אֵלֶיךָ כָּל־רִשְׁעֵי אָרֶץ.
All the inhabitants of the world will REALIZE and KNOW	32. יַכִּירוּ וְיֵדְעוּ כָּל־יוֹשְׁבֵי תֵבֵל
that every KNEE must BEND to YOU	33. כִּי לְךָ תִּכְרַע כָּל־בֶּרֶךְ
and every TONGUE must SWEAR allegiance to You (Isaiah 45:23).	34. תִּשָּׁבַע כָּל־לָשׁוֹן.
Before You ADONAI, our God,	35. לְפָנֶיךָ יְיָ אֱלֹהֵינוּ
They will BOW and LIE DOWN-in-THANKS	36. יִכְרְעוּ וְיִפֹּלוּ.
and give HONOR to Your precious NAME	37. וְלִכְבוֹד שִׁמְךָ יְקָר יִתֵּנוּ,
and they will accept on themselves	38. וִיקַבְּלוּ כֻלָּם
the YOKE-of-Your-EMPIRE	39. אֶת־עֹל מַלְכוּתֶךָ
and You will quickly RULE over them for EVER and ALWAYS,	40. וְתִמְלֹךְ עֲלֵיהֶם מְהֵרָה לְעוֹלָם וָעֶד,
BECAUSE Yours is the EMPIRE	41. כִּי הַמַּלְכוּת שֶׁלְּךָ הִיא
and You will RULE beyond forEVER in HONOR,	42. וּלְעוֹלְמֵי עַד תִּמְלוֹךְ בְּכָבוֹד,
As it is written in Your TORAH:	43. כַּכָּתוּב בְּתוֹרָתֶךָ:
"ADONAI will RULE for EVER and ALWAYS" (Exodus 15:18).	44. יְיָ יִמְלֹךְ לְעֹלָם וָעֶד.
As it is SAID:	45. וְנֶאֱמַר:
"ADONAI will be the RULER over the whole EARTH—	46. וְהָיָה יְיָ לְמֶלֶךְ עַל כָּל־הָאָרֶץ,
on that day ADONAI will be ONE	47. בַּיּוֹם הַהוּא יִהְיֶה יְיָ אֶחָד
and ADONAI's NAME will be ONE." (Zachariah 14:9).	48. וּשְׁמוֹ אֶחָד.

89

TRANSLATE וַאֲנַחְנוּ כּוֹרְעִים

This page works on the translation of וַאֲנַחְנוּ כּוֹרְעִים and a commentary.

Big Ideas

1. Growing and reinforcing Hebrew vocabulary leads to a growing affinity with the liturgy.
2. Applying the Hebrew they have to form rough translations of Hebrew prayers (a) helps students to feel closer to those texts, (b) reinforces the Hebrew they are learning and (c) develops a process they can continue to apply to the Siddur.

Learning Activities

1. Introducing/reviewing vocabulary
2. Working out a trial translation
3. Correcting translations
4. Prayer drill
5. Read the Story

You Know You've Succeeded When...

1. Students work out a reasonable translation of this text.
2. Students correct their translation.

1. Introducing/Reviewing Vocabulary ■ [a] Using VOCABULARY POSTERS and FLASHCARDS, the teacher should introduce and drill the core vocabulary needed for this translation. [b] Some game playing or team competition is the perfect way to reinforce this vocabulary.

2. Working out a Trial Translation ■ [a] Working in pairs, students should develop their own best TRANSLATION of this text. [b] They should not worry about being perfect—they should worry about coming close.

EXPECT a working translation something like:
And we knee bend and bow and bend.
Before King, King of Kings, the Holy One Bless He.

3. Correcting translations ■ Students will probably need help with:

[a] לִפְנֵי מֶלֶךְ = before THE King

4. Prayer Drill ■ Practice performing this portion of the prayer. SING or READ it together.

5. Read the Story ■ Begin reading the story "The Jewel." It continues on page 90.

TRANSLATION

Review the vocabulary and make your best guess at the meaning of this part of the עָלֵינוּ.

ruler מֶלֶךְ   face פָּנִים   thanks מוֹדֶה   bow שׁתה   bend כָּרַע

holy קדשׁ

bless ברך

Take your best guess at the meaning of this text

וַאֲנַחְנוּ כּוֹרְעִים וּמִשְׁתַּחֲוִים וּמוֹדִים

לִפְנֵי מֶלֶךְ מַלְכֵי הַמְּלָכִים הַקָּדוֹשׁ בָּרוּךְ הוּא.

➤ *And we knee bend and bow and bend.*
Before King, King of Kings, the Holy One Bless He.

word parts		words
the = הַ to/for = לְ and = וּ/וְ		He = הוּא

The Jewel

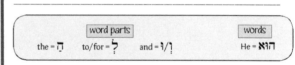

This jewel was the biggest and the best of all the jewels that came out of the mine. The king wanted it from the minute he saw it. It was the best. He had to have it. He said, "If it is the best, if it is the biggest, it is mine!"

The king gave the giant ruby to the royal jeweler. He said to him, "Polish it. Make it perfect." The jeweler put the ocular, magnifying glass, to his eye. He looked at every side of the ruby. He looked at it over and over again. Finally, in a soft and shaky voice, he said, "Your Majesty, there is a crack in this stone."

The king said, "So fix it."

The jeweler said, "I am sorry, Your Majesty, but it cannot be done."

90

The king went and got another royal jeweler. This one put in his ocular. This one also looked and looked. After a long time this one said, "Your Majesty, the best thing we can do is cut the big stone into three beautiful smaller stones. Each one of the three will be wonderful."

The king said, "Then it will not be the biggest or the best." Then the king went and got another new royal jeweler. The king got a lot of new royal jewelers because not one of them knew how to fix a crack in a large and beautiful ruby.

The king left the ruby on the table. One day a visitor came to the palace. He said, "Your Majesty, may I look at your stone?" The king gave permission. The visitor took out his ocular and looked and looked. After a long time he said, "I can make your stone into something beautiful."

The king asked, "Will it be big? Will it be beautiful? Will it be perfect?"

The visitor said, "Yes. Yes. Yes." He took the stone and went into the workshop. Everywhere in the palace you could hear the grinding and the polishing. It took three days.

The visitor came before the king with the jewel under a black cloth. The king asked, "Is it still big?" The visitor nodded. "Is it still beautiful?" The visitor nodded. "Is it perfect?" The visitor nodded. Then the king asked, "How did you get rid of the crack?"

The visitor said, "The crack is still here, Your Majesty."

The king started to say, "But, but, but, but...." when the visitor pulled the cloth off the ruby. Everyone in the palace gasped. The stone was huge. It was beautiful. And at the center of the stone was now carved a wonderful rose. The crack had become the stem.

The king opened his mouth and said, "Wow." Then the king did something unusual. He stopped talking. He just looked and looked at the jewel. Later he rewarded the jeweler. He showed everyone who came to the palace his jewel with a rose. At the end of the story the king told everyone, "I learned the most important lesson of my life that day."

Things in the kingdom were much better from that day on. (A story of the Maggid of Dubnow)

Questions

1. What do you think the rose in the ruby taught the king?
2. How is this story a story about עוֹלָם תִּקּוּן?
3. How can knowing this story help you point your heart when you say the עָלֵינוּ?

91

THE JEWEL

This story was told by Rabbi Yaakov Krantz, the Maggid of Dobnow (1741-1804). Born in a province of Vilna, Rabbi Yaakov showed exceptional homiletical and Kabbalistic talents at an early age and by the age of twenty became the *darshan* (preacher) of his city. From there he began preaching through the cities around Lublin in Poland, finally settling in Dubnow. His reputation as an outstanding maggid (preacher) spread, bringing him in contact with the great rabbis of the period, including the Vilna Gaon. The majority of his works were in homiletics, using stories and parables to transmit deeper ethical and moral teachings. This story encompasses the Lurianic idea of תִּקּוּן.

Big Ideas
1. Broken things can be fixed.
2. תִּקּוּן עוֹלָם requires each Jew to be part of the process of "healing broken-ness" and "completing creation."

Learning Activities
1. Set induction
2. Reading the story
3. Interpreting the story

You Know You've Succeeded When...
1 Students can retell this story.
2. Students can express the meaning and application of this story through answering the questions.

1. Set Induction ■ INVITE students to define תִּקּוּן עוֹלָם. EXPECT answers like "Doing good deeds." "Helping people who need help." "Taking care of the world," etc. SAY: We are now going to learn the story behind תִּקּוּן עוֹלָם.

2. Reading the Story ■ CHOOSE: [a] Read or [b] tell the story or [c] let students read it on their own.

3. Interpreting the Story ■ [a] HEVRUTA WORK: Have students work in pairs and discuss their answers to the questions. [b] CLASS WORK: Discuss and share answers to these questions.

Questions ■

1. **What do you think the rose in the ruby taught the king?** EXPECT: That things that look broken can be fixed. THIS IS A GREAT ANSWER.

2. **How is this story a story about תִּקּוּן עוֹלָם?** EXPECT: It is a story about fixing.

3. **How can knowing this story help you to point your heart when you say the עָלֵינוּ?** It helps us think about fixing.

Blank Page

קַדִּישׁ

One lesson introduces the mourners' קַדִּישׁ.

Lesson 24

Page 92: The history, forms and context of the קַדִּישׁ are introduced.

Page 93: The text and translation of the mourner's קַדִּישׁ are presented.

Page 94: We learn a little about Aramaic, the language of the קַדִּישׁ. Then we translate the first phrase of the קַדִּישׁ.

Page 95-96: The story, *A Tale of Rabbi Akiva*, presents a reason for saying קַדִּישׁ.

LESSON 23: קַדִּישׁ INTRODUCTION

This introduction describes the קַדִּישׁ.

Big Ideas

1. The קַדִּישׁ started as a study prayer.
2. The קַדִּישׁ is said seven times a day.
3. The קַדִּישׁ became a mourner's prayer helping a soul move to Gan Eden.
4. The קַדִּישׁ gathers a community and makes God feel better.

Learning Activities

1. Introducing the unit
2. Exploring the themes
3. Reviewing the key themes

You Know You've Succeeded When...

1 Students can identify the uses of the קַדִּישׁ.
2. Students can describe how קַדִּישׁ became a mourner's prayer.
3. Students can interpret the quotations from the Zohar and from Isaac Luria.

1. Introducing the Unit ■ Turn ahead to page 114. Use it to explain the text of the קַדִּישׁ.

2. Exploring the Themes ■ CONVEY THE INFORMATION IN THE INTRODUCTION: Do one of the following. [a] DESCRIBE the information to your students. [b] READ aloud and DISCUSS this information. [c] ASSIGN your students to READ the information on their own and then DISCUSS it.

3. Reviewing the Key Themes ■

a. The קַדִּישׁ is a study prayer.
b. The קַדִּישׁ is said seven times a day.
c. The קַדִּישׁ helps a soul move to Gan Eden.
d. The קַדִּישׁ gathers a community and makes God feel better.

These questions are both speculative. While there are some traditional answrs to these questions, there are no "right" answers.

Questions: How can the קַדִּישׁ move a soul to Gan Eden? How can it lift a soul to higher levels? The "traditional answer" is (as we will see in the Rabbi Akiva story that follows) that by saying קַדִּישׁ we become "good deeds" for our beloved relatives who have died.

EXPECT other answers: "By saying קַדִּישׁ we point out people to God." "We tell the people who died that we love them, and that makes their way eaiser," etc.

When the Babylonians destroyed Jerusalem and carried away all the survivors as prisoners, the Jews started *yeshivot* (Torah schools) in Babylonia. Later, when Ezra and Nehemiah organized the return to the Land of Israel, they started new *yeshivot*. No matter what difficulties they faced, no matter how sad they were, Jews gathered to study the Torah and fit it into their lives. The קַדִּישׁ started out as a prayer said at the end of study sessions. It said "God is great" and "we can find the strength to go on." (*Sotah 49a*)

Even though קַדִּישׁ is said for many other purposes, it became most famous as a prayer said by mourners. Rabbi Isaac Luria taught, "When קַדִּישׁ יָתוֹם is said for eleven months by mourners, it helps to move a soul from *Gehinom* (purgatory) to *Gan Eden* (paradise). When קַדִּישׁ is said on a *Yahrtzeit* it helps to lift a soul to higher levels of paradise."

The קַדִּישׁ is made up of ten expressions of praise. It is also a prayer that takes a minyan, a community of ten. In the *Zohar* we are taught (Aḥarei Mot), "The person for whom קַדִּישׁ is being said gets credit for gathering ten Jews." We are also told there, "The words of the קַדִּישׁ make God feel better."

Question: How can the words of the קַדִּישׁ make God feel better? The "simple answer" is that God likes praise, and this prayer praises God. But EXPECT other answers: "קַדִּישׁ is a mitzvah, and God likes it when people are doing mitzvot." "קַדִּישׁ brings Jews together, and God likes it when people gather."

קַדִּישׁ יָתוֹם

Let God's Great NAME be (1) BIG and (2) HOLY	יִתְגַּדֵּל וְיִתְקַדֵּשׁ שְׁמֵהּ רַבָּא	.1
in this world that God CREATED with will.	בְּעָלְמָא דִּי בְרָא כִרְעוּתֵהּ	.2
Let God completely RULE the EMPIRE	וְיַמְלִיךְ מַלְכוּתֵהּ	.3
in this life and in these days,	בְּחַיֵּיכוֹן וּבְיוֹמֵיכוֹן	.4
and in the lifetime of all the Families-of-Israel.	וּבְחַיֵּי דְכָל־בֵּית יִשְׂרָאֵל	.5
Let this happen QUICKLY in a nearby time	בַּעֲגָלָא וּבִזְמַן קָרִיב	.6
and let us say: "AMEN."	וְאִמְרוּ אָמֵן.	.7
Let God's Great NAME be blessed	יְהֵא שְׁמֵהּ רַבָּא מְבָרַךְ	.8
in the world and in the world of worlds—FOREVER.	לְעָלַם וּלְעָלְמֵי עָלְמַיָּא.	.9
(3) Blessed, (4) Called AMAZING, (5) Glorified	יִתְבָּרַךְ וְיִשְׁתַּבַּח וְיִתְפָּאַר	.10
(6) Extolled, (7) Honored, (8) Respected,	וְיִתְרוֹמַם וְיִתְנַשֵּׂא וְיִתְהַדָּר	.11
(9) Lifted Up and (10) HALLELUYAHed	וְיִתְעַלֶּה וְיִתְהַלָּל	.12
be the NAME of the Holy-ONE-Who-is-to-be-Blessed	שְׁמֵהּ דְּקֻדְשָׁא בְּרִיךְ הוּא	.13
above anything we can Bless and Sing	לְעֵלָּא מִן כָּל־בִּרְכָתָא וְשִׁירָתָא	.14
above all prayers and consolations	תֻּשְׁבְּחָתָא וְנֶחֱמָתָא	.15
that we can say in this world. And let us say: "AMEN."	דַּאֲמִירָן בְּעָלְמָא וְאִמְרוּ אָמֵן.	.16
Let there be a great PEACE from heaven.	יְהֵא שְׁלָמָא רַבָּא מִן שְׁמַיָּא	.17
Let us have a good life—and the same for all of Israel	וְחַיִּים עָלֵינוּ וְעַל כָּל־יִשְׂרָאֵל	.18
and let us say: "Amen."	וְאִמְרוּ אָמֵן.	.19
May the One-Who-Makes PEACE in the heavens above	עֹשֶׂה שָׁלוֹם בִּמְרוֹמָיו	.20
May that One make PEACE for us	הוּא יַעֲשֶׂה שָׁלוֹם עָלֵינוּ	.21
and for all of Israel and let us say: "AMEN."	וְעַל כָּל־יִשְׂרָאֵל וְאִמְרוּ אָמֵן.	.22

93

MOURNER'S קַדִּישׁ

This page contains the Hebrew and English text of the קַדִּישׁ blessing.

Big Ideas

1. When we enable students to perfect performances of core liturgy we make it possible for them to far more easily participate in communal worship.
2. By scanning the English of prayers students can grow insights into the meaning of the liturgy.
3. God is to be praised.

Learning Activities

1. Scanning the English text
2. Practicing the Hebrew text

You Know You've Succeeded When...

1. Students describe insights gained from looking at the English text.
2. Students practice their performance of the Hebrew text.

1. Scanning the English Text ■ INVITE students to SCAN the English translation of these prayers. ASK them what "big ideas" they can find by looking.

INSIGHTS that might be shared:

- This prayer says 9 things about God's name.
- Peace is something we want.

2. Practicing the Hebrew Text ■ [a] INVITE students to work with a partner and practice the prayer. [b] READ or SING the prayers together as a class. [c] INVITE individual students or teams of students to perform individual lines or sections.

MEET ARAMAIC/TRANSLATE FIRST FOUR WORDS

This page works on the translation of הֲשִׁיבֵנוּ and a commentary.

Big Ideas

1. Aramaic is a different language that is related to Hebrew.
2. Growing and reinforcing Hebrew vocabulary leads to a growing affinity with the liturgy.
3. Applying the Hebrew they have to form rough translations of Hebrew prayers (a) helps students to feel closer to those texts, (b) reinforces the Hebrew they are learning and (c) develops a process they can continue to apply to the Siddur.

Learning Activities

1. Meet Aramaic
2. Introducing/reviewing vocabulary
3. Working out a trial translation
4. Correcting translations
5. Prayer drill

You Know You've Succeeded When...

1. Students work out a reasonable translation of this text.
2. Students correct their translation.

1. Meet Aramaic ■ [a] READ and DISCUSS the sidebar on Aramaic. EMPHASIZE the connection to Hebrew. [b] Let students work in Hevruta or alone on the matching exercise. [c] Go over the matching exercise. EMPHASIZE that if you know Hebrew you can get a sense of Aramaic.

2. Introducing/Reviewing Vocabulary ■ [a] Using VOCABULARY POSTERS and FLASHCARDS, the teacher should introduce and drill the core vocabulary needed for this translation. [b] Some game playing or team competition is the perfect way to reinforce this vocabulary.

3. Working out a Trial Translation ■ [a] Working in pairs, students should develop their own best TRANSLATION of this text. [b] They should not worry about being perfect—they should worry about coming close.

EXPECT a working translation something like:
Big and holy the great name.

4. Correcting Translations ■

Students will probably not need much help on this translation.

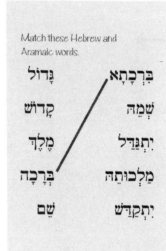

Meet Aramaic

Aramaic is a language that is connected to Arabic, Hebrew, Ethiopic, and Akkadian (ancient Babylonian and Assyrian). It is particularly closely related to Hebrew, and was written in a variety of alphabetic scripts. What we call "Hebrew" writing is actually an Aramaic script.

Aramaic is a really old language that comes from almost three thousand years ago (900-700 B.C.E.). Portions of the Bible, parts of the Books of Ezra and Daniel, are in Aramaic. Parts of the Talmud, the Midrash, and other important books are also in Aramaic. So is the קַדִּישׁ.

Match these Hebrew and Aramaic words.

גָּדוֹל	בִּרְכָתָא
קָדוֹשׁ	שְׁמֵהּ
מֶלֶךְ	יִתְגַּדַּל
בְּרָכָה	מַלְכוּתֵהּ
שֵׁם	יִתְקַדַּשׁ

TRANSLATION

Review the vocabulary and make your best guess at the meaning of this part of the קַדִּישׁ.

Your teacher will help you with your translation.

words
name = שֵׁם
great = רַבָּה

 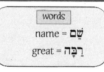

holy קדש   great נדל

יִתְגַּדַּל וְיִתְקַדַּשׁ שְׁמֵהּ רַבָּא

Big and holy the great name.

94

5. Prayer Drill ■ Practice performing this portion of the prayer. SING or READ it together.

A Tale of Rabbi Akiva

Rabbi Akiva was walking through a cemetery. He saw a naked man, covered in soot, carrying a huge bundle of wood on his head. The man was running with the load. He was shouting the Aramaic version of "I'm late. I'm late. If I don't finish they will make it worse." Rabbi Akiva asked the man, "Is there anything I can do to help? If you are poor, can I buy you out of this debt to these masters who are way too demanding?" The man said, "You are talking to a dead man. I am in *Gehinom*, the place one waits before going on to the Garden of Eden. I will be here forever. Every night they boil me in oil using the wood I collect."

Rabbi Akiva asked, "What is your name?" The man answered, "Akiva." The rabbi asked further, "What was your crime? What will help you to move on?" The man answered, "I was a tax collector, and I took bribes from the rich and taxed the poor to death to make it up. They told me that my only way out of *Gehinom* was for a child of mine to say the קַדִּישׁ. I need that child to count as one of my good deeds." In those days one said the קַדִּישׁ only at the end of Torah study. It was not a mourner's prayer. The person with the best Torah insight led it.

95

A TALE OF RABBI AKIVA

This midrash from Mahzor Vitry is the classic "origin" story for the mourner's קַדִּישׁ. It explains how a study קַדִּישׁ turned into a prayer for the dead. Its message is that we become good deeds for the people for whom we say קַדִּישׁ.

Big Ideas

1. When we say קַדִּישׁ we become "good deeds" for the people for whom we say קַדִּישׁ.
2. In doing that, it also transforms the person who says קַדִּישׁ.

Learning Activities

1. Set induction
2. Reading the story
3. Interpreting the story

You Know You've Succeeded When...

1 Students can retell this story.
2. Students can express the meaning and application of this story through answering the questions.

1. Set Induction ■ SAY: "Here is another story about reasons for saying קַדִּישׁ."

2. Reading the Story ■ CHOOSE: [a] Read or [b] tell the story or [c] let students read it on their own.

3. Interpreting the Story ■ [a] HEVRUTA WORK: Have students work in pairs and discuss their answers to the questions. [b] CLASS WORK: Discuss and share answers to these questions.

Questions ∎

1. According to this story, what does קַדִּישׁ do for the dead person? EXPECT: "It helps them get into the Garden of Eden."

2. According to this story, what does קַדִּישׁ do for the person who says it? EXPECT: "It makes them feel good." "It gives them a mitzvah to do." THESE ARE GOOD ANSWERS.

3. How can remembering this story help you to know where to point your heart when you participate in the mourner's קַדִּישׁ? It lets us focus on the person for whom we are saying קַדִּישׁ when we pray.

Rabbi Akiva left Akiva and went looking for a child. He found a son. The son was living as a non-Jew. He did not know even one Hebrew letter. The Jewish community had abandoned him. Rabbi Akiva began to teach him, but the son's heart was not in his studies. Rabbi Akiva tried all his best teacher tricks—nothing worked.

Rabbi Akiva prayed to God and asked for the child's heart to be opened.

Slowly the lessons went better. Once, when Rabbi Akiva brought the son to a Torah study, the son was picked to lead the קַדִּישׁ. When the prayer was over, Akiva went to the Garden of Eden.

That night Rabbi Akiva had a dream. In the dream he heard Akiva's voice. "You saved me from *Gehinom*. May your soul go quickly to the Garden of Eden in its time." In his dream, Rabbi Akiva said, "Eternal, Your NAME lasts forever, Your MEMORY is for all generations" (Ps 102.13). This is when the mourner's קַדִּישׁ began (*Maḥzor Vitry*).

▶ Questions
1. According to this story, what does the קַדִּישׁ do for the dead person?
2. According to this story, what does the קַדִּישׁ do for the person who says it?
3. How can remembering this story help you know where to point your heart when you participate in the mourner's קַדִּישׁ?

96

Blank Page

97